Communications
in Computer and Information Science 1617

More information about this series at https://link.springer.com/bookseries/7899

Christian Zirpins · Guadalupe Ortiz et al. (Eds.)

Advances in Service-Oriented and Cloud Computing

International Workshops of ESOCC 2022
Wittenberg, Germany, March 22–24, 2022
Revised Selected Papers

 Springer

Editors
Christian Zirpins (iD)
Karlsruhe University of Applied Sciences
Karlsruhe, Germany

Guadalupe Ortiz (iD)
University of Cádiz
Cádiz, Spain

Workshop Editors *see next page*

ISSN 1865-0929   ISSN 1865-0937 (electronic)
Communications in Computer and Information Science
ISBN 978-3-031-23297-8   ISBN 978-3-031-23298-5 (eBook)
https://doi.org/10.1007/978-3-031-23298-5

This Springer imprint is published by the registered company Springer Nature Switzerland AG
The registered company address is: Gewerbestrasse 11, 6330 Cham, Switzerland

Workshop Editors

AWACS

Zoltan Nochta ⓘ
Karlsruhe University of Applied Sciences
Karlsruhe, Germany

Oliver Waldhorst ⓘ
Karlsruhe University of Applied Sciences
Karlsruhe, Germany

PhD Symposium

Jacopo Soldani ⓘ
University of Pisa
Pisa, Italy

Massimo Villari ⓘ
University of Messina
Messina, Italy

Project-Track

Damian Tamburri ⓘ
TU/e – JADS
Eindhoven, The Netherlands

Preface

The European Conference on Service-Oriented and Cloud Computing (ESOCC) is among the leading events on advancing the state of the art in services and cloud technologies. It serves as an important venue for scientists as well as practitioners from academia and industry. The main objective of the event is to provide a broad forum for the exchange of ideas. In this respect, workshops are an important part of the conference. They contribute to an intensive exchange in special fields of service-oriented and cloud computing.

In addition, ESOCC includes a PhD Symposium where PhD students can present their ideas and results, ranging from early ideas to almost completed work. Another part of ESOCC is the Projects Track that addresses recent developments from collaborative research projects. Finally, the ESOCC Industrial Track is a forum for the latest achievements of industrial research and development. The workshop proceedings volume of ESOCC 2022 contains contributions from the following workshops and events:

- First International Workshop on AI for Web Application Infrastructure and Cloud Platform Security (AWACS 2022)
- ESOCC 2022 PhD Symposium
- ESOCC 2022 Projects Track
- ESOCC 2022 Industrial Track

We are grateful to Wolf Zimmermann and his team for the excellent organization. They made it possible to successfully hold the conference in a virtual form despite all of the worries and restrictions of the ongoing pandemic situation in spring 2022. We also thank the organizers and Program Committee members of the workshops. Their efforts enabled an attractive program. Finally, we thank the authors who submitted their contributions to the workshops, the presenters, and the attendees. Without their support, active and fruitful workshops would not be possible.

March 2022

Guadalupe Ortiz
Christian Zirpins

Organization

General Chair

Wolf Zimmermann   Martin Luther University Halle-Wittenberg, Germany

Program Chairs

Fabrizio Montesi   University of Southern Denmark, Denmark
George Papadopoulos   University of Cyprus, Cyprus

Workshop Chairs

Guadalupe Ortiz   University of Cadiz, Spain
Christian Zirpins   Karlsruhe University of Applied Sciences, Germany

Steering Committee

Antonio Brogi   University of Pisa, Italy
Schahram Dustdar   TU Wien, Austria
Paul Grefen   Eindhoven University of Technology, The Netherlands
Einar Broch Johnson   University of Oslo, Norway
Kyriakos Kritikos   ICS-FORTH, Greece
Winfried Lamersdorf   University of Hamburg, Germany
Flavio de Paoli   University of Milano-Bicocca, Italy
Ernesto Pimentel   University of Malaga, Spain
Pierluigi Plebani   Politecnico di Milano, Italy
Ulf Schreier   Hochschule Furtwangen University, Germany
Stefan Schulte   TU Wien, Austria
Massimo Villari   University of Messina, Italy
Olaf Zimmermann   HSR FHO Rapperswil, Switzerland
Wolf Zimmermann   Martin Luther University Halle-Wittenberg, Germany

Contents

ESOCC 2022 Industrial Track

First International Workshop on AI for Web Application Infrastructure and Cloud Platform Security (AWACS 2022)

Preface to the AWACS 2022 Workshop

In recent decades, cloud computing has enabled the rapid proliferation of web-based information systems that are delivered as services, eliminating the need to purchase and maintain expensive or sophisticated hardware for data storage and processing. Cloud computing systems have therefore minimized the upfront investment of service users while promising high availability, scalability, and elasticity on demand, as well as high levels of performance, fault tolerance, and security. Artificial intelligence (AI) and machine learning (ML) techniques can help DevOps and SecOps teams run cloud services and the underlying web-based information systems in a highly secure and efficient manner. They can gain an accurate and comprehensive understanding of security incidents along the entire system stack, such as unexpected application performance degradation due to network attacks or malicious end-user activity, and proactively initiate appropriate countermeasures. Current AI- and ML-based approaches and tools mainly focus on detecting and mitigating attacks in isolated technical domains and layers, while attacks on web-based services often leave traces throughout the system. AI-based cross-domain attack detection and orchestrated mitigation therefore have the potential to improve the capabilities of security and risk management systems overall.

The International Workshop on AI for Web Application Infrastructure and Cloud Platform Security (AWACS 2022) was organized out of the project Artificial Intelligence in Secure Web Infrastructures with Digital Identity Management funded by the German Federal Ministry of Education and Research. AWACS 2022 focused on the general applicability and integration of AI/ML methods in the field of security and risk management in the context of modern web-based information systems and brought together researchers both from academia and industry. Originally planned to be held co-located with ESOCC 2022 in Wittenberg, Germany, AWACS 2022 was held as a virtual event on March 22, 2022, due to the COVID-19 pandemic.

The workshop received six full paper submissions. All papers were reviewed by three or more members of the Program Committee in a single blind review process to ensure high quality. Finally, three papers were selected for presentation.

The workshop opened with a keynote talk by Ulf Brackmann (Vice President, Artificial Intelligence Technology, SAP) on "Enterprise AI and Embedded AI by SAP". A lively discussion following the talk showed the relevance of the topic for the audience present. Afterwards, in the technical session, the three selected papers on data governance, secure peer-to-peer federated learning, and AI-based network attack detection were presented. The session included the presentations "Towards a Metadata Management System for provenance, reproducibility and accountability in Federated Machine Learning" by José Antonio Peregrina Pérez, "Towards a Secure Peer-to-Peer Federated Learning Framework" by Tim Piotrowski, and "MIDA: Micro-Flow Independent Detection of DDoS Attacks with CNNs" by Samuel Kopmann.

The AWACS co-organizers thank all Program Committee members, authors, and presenters for making AWACS 2022 a success. We look forward to the next edition of AWACS.

June 2022   Zoltán Nochta
                                                                                          Oliver P. Waldhorst

Organization

Workshop Co-organizers

Jürgen Angele	adesso SE, Germany
Jan Griebsch	1&1 IONOS SE, Germany
Martin Johns	TU Braunschweig, Germany
Zoltán Nochta	SAP, Germany
Oliver Waldhorst	Karlsruhe University of Applied Sciences, Germany
Christian Zirpins	Karlsruhe University of Applied Sciences, Germany
Martina Zitterbart	Karlsruhe Institute of Technology, Germany

Program Committee

Hannes Federrath	University of Hamburg, Germany
Dieter Fensel	University of Innsbruck, Austria
Martin Härterich	SAP, Germany
Sigfried Handschuh	University St. Gallen, Switzerland
Hans-Joachim Hof	Technische Hochschule Ingolstadt, Germany
Boris Koldehofe	University of Groningen, Netherlands
Heiko Koziolek	ABB, Germany
Andreas Oberweis	Karlsruhe Institute of Technology, Germany
Joachin Posegga	University of Passau, Germany
Konrad Rieck	Technical University of Braunschweig, Germany
Daniel Schlör	University of Würzburg, Germany
Christian Wressnegger	Karlsruhe Institute of Technology, Germany

Additional Reviewers

Elif Bilge Kavun	University of Passau, Germany

Towards a Metadata Management System for Provenance, Reproducibility and Accountability in Federated Machine Learning

José A. Peregrina[1,2]([✉]), Guadalupe Ortiz[1], and Christian Zirpins[2]

[1] Computer Science and Engineering Department, University of Cádiz,
Av. Universidad de Cádiz, 10, 11519 Puerto Real, Cádiz, Spain
`guadalupe.ortiz@uca.es`
[2] Faculty of Computer Science and Business Information Systems,
Karlsruhe University of Applied Sciences,
Moltkestr. 30, 76133 Karlsruhe, Germany
{`jose_antonio.peregrina_perez`,`christian.zirpins`}`@h-ka.de`

Abstract. The application of Data Governance (DG) to Federated Machine Learning (FML) could provide a way to produce better Machine Learning models. Nevertheless, such an application is still almost nonexistent in literature. Within a proposal for applying DG to FML, we first present an approach of metadata for FML, to provide accountability and assist with the continuous improvement of models in the federation. Our proposal includes a metadata model for tracing the operations of participants and collecting all information regarding the definition of goals and configuration of FML training processes. Additionally, we present the outline of a metadata management system as part of a broader DG architecture. Finally, we show some use cases of metadata management.

Keywords: Federated Machine Learning · Data Governance · Metadata

1 Introduction

Federated Machine Learning (FML) is becoming increasingly popular, as it circumvents data protection regulations, allowing the training of a machine learning (ML) model on unseen data. This is especially useful when the data is of sensitive nature (like some personal data that allow to uniquely identify a person), since it is not allowed to share such data with another organization. However, although FML presents a solution for the problem of lacking data, it comes along with other challenges. Among the multiple scenarios of FML, cross-silo scenarios are those where the participants belong to different organizations, possessing high amounts of data [9]. However, FML requires the participants to agree on which data will be used, which kind of ML model will be produced and the standards of quality that such a model must accomplish. Producing an ML model on first

C. Zirpins et al. (Eds.): ESOCC 2022 Workshops, CCIS 1617, pp. 5–18, 2022.
https://doi.org/10.1007/978-3-031-23298-5_1

try, that accomplishes all of this, is not usually feasible. Moreover, there can be participants that do not provide a sufficient amount of good data, but still try to receive a trained model. For these reasons, some mechanisms to support FML are desirable, in order to ensure that participants receive a model suitable for their needs in a safe and balanced training environment.

In pursuance of such mechanisms, Data Governance (DG) appears as a promising approach. DG covers activities to ensure the correct and responsible management of data, with a definition of different responsibilities among the actors participating in the system. Nevertheless, the application of DG to artificial intelligence (AI), and specially to FML, is not trivial. Some works [4,8] have already studied what needs to be done to govern AI. Nevertheless, neither of them proposed the design or implementation of a system to manage the governing process as such. Moreover, the mentioned works focus on ML, not on FML, what would require to cover additional aspects in terms of what is shared among different participants. Therefore, work in the conception of a system to enable AI governance in FML environments still remains to be seen.

One important aspect in governance is the use of metadata to support other mechanisms. Metadata, commonly known as "data that refers to data", allows to cover auxiliary information regarding the different assets being governed. For example, it can inform about the provenance of data, or show who was responsible for the training of a model. When it comes to ML, tools like *TensorFlow Extended Metadata* allow to store metadata regarding the configuration of an experiment. Another example is *ArangoML* that provides a graph database to store information about the configuration of a training process. From another perspective, blockchains have been proposed to store metadata for provenance and accountability. For example, [6] provides an architecture for decentralized learning that stores metadata in the ledger regarding which nodes, that represent participants either providing models or data, have participated in the process. However, such proposals do not seem to specify, which metadata must be stored for an efficient analysis and reproducibility.

To the best of our knowledge, there is currently no proposal for a metadata system supporting DG in cross-silo FML. Additionally, we would like to mention that our model can also be applied to cross-device scenarios, although our focus remains on cross-silo, as we disregard factors like resources of the devices, connection stability, etc. To this end, our proposal aims at the following two goals: (1) enable accountability within a federation and (2) provide means of reproducibility and assessment, in order to allow participants to work effectively towards the improvement of an ML model by means of federated training. Therefore, the contributions of this paper are:

- A *metadata model* for storing a trace of the operations in a federation and the results of the training process
- A *metadata management system* to control all FML metadata that is integrated with other governance components and general FML architecture

The rest of the paper is structured as follows. Section 2 introduces the background of FML, DG and ML metadata. Section 3 surveys related approaches and tooling. Section 4 discusses requirements to be fulfilled by an FML-adapted metadata management system. Section 5 presents the conception of a metadata model for FML. Section 6 introduces our metadata management system and the role it plays in a holistic FML-architecture. Section 7 presents a demonstration of use cases. Finally, Sect. 8 ends with conclusions and future work.

2   Background

The following section presents the background of our proposal. Subsection 2.1 introduces the concept of FML in different scenarios. Subsection 2.2 explains the concept of DG, and its application to AI. Finally, Subsect. 2.3 portrays how to measure the quality of models and data adapted to the FML scenarios.

2.1   Federated Machine Learning

FML is a recent technology to train ML models with unseen data from different sources without having to move such data from where it is stored. The only artefacts that are exchanged are the models. One of the first examples of this is the training performed by Google for GBoard [7]. Here, FML was used to train an ML model for predictive text functionality in GBoard, a software keyboard for smartphones. The process is the following: First, a server initializes the model. After this, the model is sent to the participants of the training. Such participants in this use case are the phones of the users. Once the participants receive the model, it is trained with the local data of the device. Once it is trained and depending on the aggregation process, either the gradient [17] or the weights [12] are sent to the server. When the server has received them all, it aggregates them into a single one. This process is repeated until the aggregated ML model achieves an acceptable accuracy. Thanks to this procedure, the data never leaves the individual devices, increasing the security of the process.

There are different categories of FML, depending on how the training data is organized [21]. In Horizontal Federated Learning, the training data of the participants contain the same features, but the instances of the data are different. In Vertical Federated Learning, the datasets have different features, but entities appear as instances in the different datasets (such entities can be persons, devices, etc). Last, Federated Transfer Learning intends to train a model that learns a common representation between two feature sets. In this work, we focus on the first representation.

FML can also be classified in two different scenarios, depending on the characteristics of the participants [9]. In a Cross-silo Federated Learning scenario, the number of participants tends to be small, yet they possess high amounts of data and there are no continuous disconnections from the side of the participants, therefore they can be always relied upon for the training process. In a Cross-Device Federated Learning scenario, there are usually more data sources, but they can disconnect and reappear at any time in the federation. This scenario was the one that Google presented with GBoard, where the data sources were the phones of the users. This proposal focuses on the first scenario.

2.2   Data Governance

DG has been characterized as the different activities in charge of ensuring the correct management of data, the definition of responsibilities of the agents involved in such processes and the monitoring of all the actions performed to ensure the compliance of such activities [8]. Kathri et al. [10] proposed five domains as a reference to design DG. The first domain is Data Principles, which serves to define all the aimed uses for the data, and the responsibilities behind the people managing such data. Second is Data Quality, defining the quality standards of the different elements. The third domain is Metadata, that are all the data that describe the data being managed. Such metadata can store information about who performed a certain operation in the system, or descriptions about the data helping other people inside the system to understand it. Fourth is the domain of Data Access that defines the different procedures for access control within the federation, and the procedure to allow for external audits. Last domain is the Data Life Cycle, which defines how data must be managed during the time it is stored in the system.

When applying DG to AI, raw data is not the only thing to control. It is also necessary to control the quality of the ML models produced (though, from a fundamental perspective, this is data as well). Mapping from the aforementioned dimensions, the Data Principles define the goals that a model must achieve. Data Quality defines standards that the model needs to achieve. In this case, we will introduce them later on. Metadata concern all information regarding characteristics of the model and the training process. Data Access controls, who has access to the model. Finally, the Data Life Cycle controls, how long the model will be stored. Such storage can go beyond its use for inference, as the model can be applied for comparisons. For example, in the case of a model for healthcare, the principles could match the goal of the classification of the model. The quality could describe the accuracy that the model needs to achieve. Also, it could be required to explain, how it reached a decision. The metadata stored can be related to the training process, for instance the data that was used and the person responsible of the training. The data access can be related to whom access to the model has been granted and the information related to it. Finally, the data life-cycle could involve how to store the model for both predictions and comparisons with new developed models.

2.3   ML Metadata Management

Metadata in ML is usually related to storage and management of information regarding various aspects of ML. E.g., information regarding the training configuration, like data used, the algorithm used or responsible agent of the training process. Our goals behind storing metadata are to achieve a higher quality for ML models and provide accountability functionalities in the federation.

As regards quality, this is usually referred to in the literature as "fitness for use" [19]. For both models and data, those of the best quality are those that solve the problem in the best way, attending to the needs of the participants.

Part of this research has been performed by Siebert et al. [16], who have proposed a model for ML quality assessment. Because there can be multiple use cases and elements that affect the ML training process, there must be a way of keeping information about the effects of different changes. Provenance metadata is usually used in data science workflows [18], to store different parameters of the training, so the resultant models can be compared based on the changes.

As regards accountability, this is especially needed in an environment with participants that do not trust each other. Achieving accountability means having information on the responsible authors of different activities [14] in case they cause any harm. This way, explanations can be requested from these authors.

3   Related Work

DG for AI has been discussed by Jannsen et al. [8]. In this work, a procedure for effectively governing AI models is proposed, where multiple assessments are being run throughout the training process, as well as continuous monitoring during the inference process. Chandrasekaran et al. [4] shows a comprehensive literature review of different proposals for governing AI. Nevertheless, these two works focus only on governance for AI, without proposing anything specifically for FML. Also, there are no approaches for systems that could enforce this governance. Some other works have focused only on certain aspects of governance for ML models. Accountability in FML has been studied by Balta et al. [2]. They consider the inclusion of an external agent that audits the resultant model.

In terms of metadata used for governance, it is a common approach to add blockchain technology to the FML process for accountability purposes. For example, FLChain [13] presented the use of Hyperledger Fabric, to have some means of provenance for the FML process. BlockFLA [5] uses a public and private blockchain for tamper-proof provenance, therefore adding accountability to the process. Substra [6] provides a blockchain in its architecture in order to store, who was involved in a training process. It is worth mentioning that none of the proposals focused on the format of the metadata with the exception of [14], which proposes an ontology for accountability in FML. In terms of reproducibility of experiments, there are approaches for ML, like the one from Souza et al. [18] that uses PROV for storing all the configuration of the training process. Tools like *ArangoML Pipeline* [15] and *TensorFlow Metadata Extended*[1] can track metadata regarding the configuration of the training process. This helps to collect insights in how the training should be configured for future training processes. Nevertheless, none of the proposals provide comprehensive metadata for governance. Our system collects both, metadata regarding the configuration of the training, like information about the models chosen as well as data formats; and metadata regarding who performed the different operations in the federation, enabling accountability in the process.

---

[1] https://www.tensorflow.org/tfx/guide/mlmd.

4   FML Metadata Management

Among all the different uses of metadata, our proposal focuses on two that we consider essential to support governance in FML: 1) to store former configurations and results from the training processes, and 2) to trace the authorship of operations from different participants. In the literature, there is currently no proposal that achieves these two aspects as the adaption towards a federation may involve hiding some information that other proposals would include within the gathered metadata.

On the one hand, achieving a high-quality model is an iterative process of optimization in terms of parameter configuration. To this end, possessing a history of values for different parameters becomes essential, allowing for continuous improvement over the FML training process. Nevertheless, in an FML scenario, direct access to these elements is mostly not possible. Therefore, a privacy-preserving representation of these elements, that still provides the participants with enough information to understand their characteristics, must be achieved.

On the other hand, there must be a trace of all the operations, to hold the responsible participants of those actions accountable. This is important, because the participants may only trust each other to a certain degree. Additionally, they may introduce operations that end up worsening the model. Even if there is no intention to harm, the participant should still give an explanation on why she made such a decision. Therefore, all the operations must be traceable back to the ones who performed them.

5   Metadata for Governance in FML

The following section contains an overview of the metadata model being developed for the FML Governance system. Both the full model and comprehensive descriptions for each element are presented.

To apply DG to FML, the use of metadata becomes necessary. On the one hand, as there are multiple participants involved, everyone is interested in knowing that the others are acting honestly. For example, some participants may want to push a specific model, because they would benefit from it. However, it would come at the expense of the rest of the participants. In order to do so, they may decide to underperform in other configurations [11]. Another example may be the inclusion of a feature that could be used for adversarial attacks on tabular data [1]. On the other hand, it is important to have the ability to make a precise assessment on what are the consequences of the decisions in the federation. For this, the model aims to cover two main aspects: providing information about training processes and tracing the operations performed.

The model was designed using PROV[2], which provides functionality to trace the participants responsible for the operations performed. Then, within this model, the entities are configured to store information regarding the training processes and their results. The model is shown in Fig. 1.

---

[2] https://www.w3.org/TR/prov-overview/.

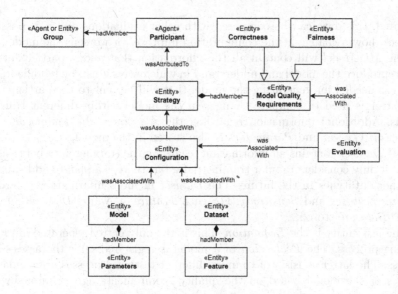

Fig. 1. Overview of the metadata model

As a starting point, participants are organized into groups. For each group, the metadata model stores the people in the group at a given moment. This is performed to maintain a trace of accountability, as it enables to know who participated in a specific training process. Then each participant is also stored with the information to identify him/her. Both of these are used as agents in the metadata model. This way, the rest of the operations can be traced back to them, enabling accountability.

The rest of the elements in the model are entities, which aim to provide retrospective information regarding former configurations of FML training processes. All entities posses an *ID*, a *Name* and a *Description*. The first entity created by a federation is the *Strategy* as it is the one defining the intended goal of the federation. Besides, it also contains the different *Model Quality Requirements* that the participants may agree upon.

The *Model Quality Requirements* currently supported are of *Correctness* and *Fairness* types. The first measures how well the model approximates the real value in terms of regression, or how well it classifies instances for classification problems. The second measures any sign of bias in the model. A bias in ML can be represented as a correlation between a feature and the target label, that is in some way harmful to users or misleading for the model. For that, the model considers the inclusion of metrics for the calculation of group fairness.

Once the group has agreed on a *Strategy* and some *Model Quality Requirements*, different configurations for the FML training process can be proposed. A configuration is formed by a *ML Model* and a *Dataset*. Once the configuration has been set, the FML training process is performed using an ML model and a dataset that match the ones in the configuration. Once the model is trained and evaluated, this data can be compared with other evaluations and it is possible to check, how a change in the configuration improves or worsens the model.

The *ML Model* will contain all the information that allows participants to both reproduce the model and understand in which ways it can be modified. The former is needed for generating the model that will be sent to the participants. The latter is used to compare changes in the model within different training rounds. Additional information regarding the *Algorithm*, the *Framework*, the *FrameworkVersion* and *Parameters* is also stored in the model.

The *Dataset* contains all information regarding the training data being used. So far, it only considers tabular training data, but there is a plan to add support for other datatypes in the future. The *Dataset* includes information regarding its *Size*, *Features* and *Sensitivity*. For each *Feature*, a *Name*, *Description* and *TypeOfData* are stored.

The last entity is the *Evaluation*. This is the only entity generated after the training process. The *Evaluation* of a model is registered after the assessment process. The latter consists of running different testing processes or calculating metrics of the model based on the quality requirements agreed upon by the participants. Nevertheless, the system does not perform such assessments itself. It only stores the results of the process. At this moment, the information contains the value of the metrics created for quality and the Shapley Values of the clients. Shapley Values [20] is a concept from Game Theory, in which the contributions of participants are analysed based on a cooperative game. In this case, the game is considered the training process. This allows to analyze the different participants with respect to the value of their contribution (i.e. data) within the training.

Overall, the metadata model stores the metadata needed to be shared, in order to enable the training process. Still, some privacy concerns may appear in two different parts of our model. The first relates to the dataset description. Specially in categorical features, sharing valid values over the participants entails that such participants have data instances with such values, which may lead to privacy concerns from their side. The other problem appears with respect to Shapley Values computation, which requires not to use secure aggregation. This can increase the threat of reconstruction attacks. Regarding the rest of the model, we consider that all the metadata stored here is the minimum needed to successfully design the federated training process, while also respecting the current data protection regulation applying at the moment. Just in the case of cross-device FML, where the coordinator has the full control over the data being used in each of the devices, it is worth considering the exclusion of this metadata model for the sake of privacy.

6   Metadata Management System

The following section introduces the metadata management system. Section 6.1 first introduces a bit of the DG architecture, and the role that the metadata system plays in it. Then, Sect. 6.2 goes into detail regarding the implementation of the metadata management system.

6.1   Architecture View

The metadata management system is part of a more general architecture, meant to support the DG processes described in Sect. 4. This section introduces the architecture of our metadata management system within a draft of the planned architecture for DG. It will also introduce some information about the operations that are enabled by the full architecture. The architecture components allow participants to agree on federated training configurations as well as on goals to assess whether the produced model possesses sufficient quality. A draft of the architecture for DG is shown in Fig. 2. Nevertheless, the latter is not in the main scope of this paper, so just a rough sketch will be given.

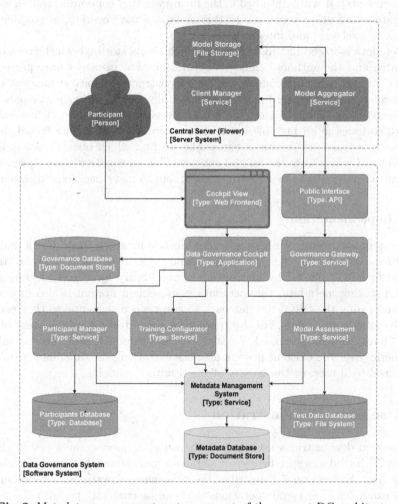

Fig. 2. Metadata management system as part of the current DG architecture

The metadata management system (highlighted in green) is connected to almost any other component within the DG architecture, as its main job is to collect all the metadata generated by such components. For instance, the system collects metadata regarding who initiated operations from both the *Participant Manager* and the *Data Governance Cockpit*. Then, from the *Data Governance Cockpit*, the *Training Configurator* and the *Model Assessment*, the system takes all metadata regarding how the training was agreed upon by the participants.

Despite the metadata management system is aimed to store governance metadata, which cannot be found elsewhere (like strategies, proposals of configurations and group management related metadata), it is possible to find similar metadata being stored in other tools (especially the metadata for reproduction of experiments). It will be studied in the future whether communication between our system and other tools, where this metadata may overlap, is possible for alignment, exchange and integration.

Metadata is stored in PROV format, which allows storing both the metadata generated and the authors behind its generation. The elements were presented in Sect. 5. This way, any component can reconstruct any entity that was used in a former process. Regarding the authors, they can be either participants or a software agents (for instance, the *Model Assessment* component). Because it is hard to imagine all possible harmful operations, and therefore forbid them, possessing a trace of operations can enable to find which operations caused a problem and which were the related entities. This information can be presented to involved participants in order to enable them to make decisions in response.

6.2   Implementation

The system is currently built as a Python library, in which the different entities are simulated to be received by other components. Then, each entity is transformed to PROV-JSON, by making use of the library for PROV documents[3]. Beyond storing metadata, the metadata management system is also in charge of transforming the PROV format back to governance elements, so they can be used by other components. For this, individual converters for each element of the model have been programmed. Finally, it is also responsible of allowing different queries over the existent provenance, like extracting the different operations performed by a user, or the quality of the resultant model.

7   Use Case Demonstration

This section demonstrates use cases of the metadata management system. Subsection 7.1 introduces specific uses of metadata and shows what can be retrieved by the user. Subsection 7.2 describes the experimental settings. Subsection 7.3 shows examples of retrieval operations that can be currently performed.

---

[3] https://prov.readthedocs.io/en/latest/.

7.1   Metadata Uses

A first use of the metadata management system is for accountability. For each operation, information is stored regarding *author* (Actor), *operation* (Activity) performed and *entities* (Entity) created. The system also stores a timestamp of the operation. This information is retrieved and transformed into *PROV-N*. Then, it can be simply printed in different ways, in order to show it to human users. Additionally, a computation of Shapley Values is stored, which allows to understand who is providing the best data for the training, or who is not adding sufficient value. Such assessment over the value can then be crossed with policies like the obligation that anyone must provide valuable data. Put differently, no one should provide irrelevant data with the aim to get an ML model without contributing to the process. Different informed actions can then be carried by other participants of the federation, or other components of the DG system.

Our second use case is a comparison among different training configurations. Any change in the training process, from the data used to the algorithm or the parameters, can change the performance of the model. Therefore, being able to reproduce the setup of a training process is essential. It helps in understanding how changes on it have improved or worsened the model. This allows for informed decisions on how the next training process should be modified.

7.2   Experiment Settings

For demonstration, a simulation of the operations within the main file of the metadata system has been performed. The training process is carried out in Flower [3], which is connected to the system by using the library and the framework in the same executable. Then, operations of configuration are simulated and the training process (based on the Flower example) is modified accordingly. After the training has been executed, the resulting value of each participant is computed and stored. All results are printed to the terminal. After the first configuration, a second is performed, improving the results of the former one.

A total of four participants are simulated here. Each of them makes a certain operation and then an operation report is printed for the first participant. The list of the operations simulated is the following:

1. Participant 1 creates a group, containing Participant 1 and 2.
2. Participant 3 and 4 join the group.
3. Participant 1 creates a simulated strategy.
4. Participant 3 proposes a dataset (in this case CIFAR10).
5. Participant 4 proposes a MobileNetV2 Deep Neural Network (DNN). The participant also proposes the parameters of the DNN.
6. The evaluation is carried and sent to the metadata management system.
7. The accuracy and Shapley Values are computed and shown to participants.
8. As the accuracy achieved is too low, Participant 2 proposes a new DNN, using *Pytorch*.
9. The evaluation of the new configuration is performed, and both the accuracy and the Shapley Values are shown to the participants.

The selection of an image dataset follows the reproduction of the example given by the Flower framework. Because the metadata model does not completely contemplate image dataset descriptions, the fields have been limited to name and description, being the description field the one that stores the majority of the needed information to put together the dataset.

7.3   Assessment of Uses

We provide a simple evaluation of the use cases by printing the different operations of a participant. This shows that a user can check, which operations were performed in the federation. A change in the proposal, that worsens the resultant model can be tracked to the responsible participant. This functionality can not provide accountability by itself, but it can definitely support accountability mechanisms and relevant information, in order to start a discussion over strange decisions being performed by a participant. The resulting report is shown in Listing 1.

Listing 1. Activity tracing report

```
==================================================
All operations performed by first_participant
==================================================
Activities related to Group
==================================================
activity(gov_prov:creation, 2022-01-02T09:01:46,
    2022-01-02T09:01:46)
--------------------------------------------------
entity(gov_prov:group_v1,
    [gov_prov:group_name="Test group",
    gov_prov:group_description="Group for testing"])
```

```
entity(gov_prov:members_1,
    [prov:type="gov_prov:participant_First_P",
    prov:type='prov:Collection'])

Activities related to Strategy
==================================================
activity(gov_prov:creation, 2022-01-02T09:01:46,
    2022-01-02T09:01:46)
--------------------------------------------------
entity(gov_prov:strategy_v1,
    [gov_prov:strategy_name="Neural network for image
    classification.", gov_prov:strategy_description=
    "The goal is achieving a good ML model,
    that can accurately identify different objects."])
```

The second part of the evaluation shows the output of the Shapley Values computation on the terminal (see Listing 2). This allows to check, which participant has contributed the lowest value. It is also possible to discern whether his participation has even worsened the model. A lower value will reflect a lower quality of the data being used. Currently, only accuracy was considered for the Shapley Values computation.

Listing 2. Training report

```
==================================================
Training report
==================================================
Name: Training report of configuration conf1
Description: Training report for the last configuration
```

```
Configuration id: conf1
Quality result of metric gov_prov:quality_result_Accuracy:
    0.10000000149011612
Shapley value of client First_P: 0.014257812712457962
Shapley value of client Second_P: 0.014257812712457962
Shapley value of client Third_P: 0.014257812712457962
Shapley value of client Fourth_P: 0.014257812712457962
```

Listing 3 correspond to an equivalent calculation of accuracy and Shapley Values, but for the second configuration. This training round achieves a better accuracy, and also shows more distinct differences among the Shapley Values of the participants. In comparison with the former, this may be due to the very low accuracy of the model. The algorithm did not allow to precisely calculate how much each participant contributes, as there was no improvement during the federated averaging process.

Listing 3. Second training report

```
===================================================
Training report
===================================================
Name: Training report of configuration conf2
Description: Training report for the second configuration
```

```
Configuration id: conf2
Quality result of metric gov_prov:quality_result_Accuracy:
    0.4018
Shapley value of client First_P: 0.05992832031249998
Shapley value of client Third_P: 0.06068593750000001
Shapley value of client Second_P: 0.059914453125
Shapley value of client Fourth_P: 0.0490541015625
```

We plan to also consider other ways to evaluate the model and thereby the training data. Also, additional applications of Shapley Values will be studied.

8   Conclusions and Future Work

In this work a metadata model and a metadata management system are proposed. The metadata model allows to comply with the main requirements of FML: 1) the tracking of experiments and 2) the accountability aspect by including the author of the different actions in the federation. The metadata management system will be integrated within the scope of a broader FML platform. We demonstrated that it is possible to retrieve all the operations performed by a specific participant. This also showed the quality achieved by the federated model and how much each participant has contributed in the training process. The proposal focuses on cross-silo scenarios, but it can also be applied to cross-device scenarios up to a certain extent. Cross-device scenarios need to take into account other factors, like resources of the devices, connection stability, etc.; this research does focus into those factors. In regards to the structure of the data, we focus as well on horizontal FML. Vertical FML is not clear for us to make a good assessment in this scenario.

Future work will focus on multiple areas. In terms of the model, information regarding agreements among the participants will be added. In terms of the system, a REST-API will be provided for integration. Based on this, we will evaluate other non-functional characteristics of the system like its efficiency in terms of calls processed or size of metadata.

Acknowledgment. Funded by the German Federal Ministry of Education and Research. Project name: KIWI, RefNr: 16KIS1142K.

References

1. Ballet, V., Renard, X., Aigrain, J., et al.: Imperceptible adversarial attacks on tabular data. arXiv:1911.03274 [cs, stat] (2019). http://arxiv.org/abs/1911.03274
2. Balta, D., et al.: Accountable federated machine learning in government: engineering and management insights. In: Edelmann, N., et al. (eds.) ePart 2021. LNCS, vol. 12849, pp. 125–138. Springer, Cham (2021). https://doi.org/10.1007/978-3-030-82824-0_10
3. Beutel, D.J., Topal, T., Mathur, A., et al.: Flower: a friendly federated learning research framework. arXiv preprint arXiv:2007.14390 (2020)
4. Chandrasekaran, V., Jia, H., Thudi, A., et al.: SoK: machine learning governance (2021). http://arxiv.org/abs/2109.10870

5. Desai, H.B., Ozdayi, M.S., Kantarcioglu, M.: BlockFLA: accountable federated learning via hybrid blockchain architecture, pp. 101–112. ACM (2021)
6. Galtier, M.N., Marini, C.: Substra: a framework for privacy-preserving, traceable and collaborative ml (2019). https://arxiv.org/abs/1910.11567
7. Hard, A., Rao, K., Mathews, R., et al.: Federated learning for mobile keyboard prediction (2018). http://arxiv.org/abs/1811.03604
8. Janssen, M., Brous, P., Estevez, E., et al.: Data governance: organizing data for trustworthy artificial intelligence. GIQ **37**(3), 101493 (2020)
9. Kairouz, P., McMahan, H.B., Avent, B., et al.: Advances and open problems in federated learning. Found. Trends ML **14**(1–2), 1–210 (2021)
10. Khatri, V., Brown, C.V.: Designing data governance. CACM **53**(1), 148–152 (2010)
11. Lin, J., Du, M., Liu, J.: Free-riders in Federated Learning: attacks and Defenses. Technical report arXiv:1911.12560 (2019). http://arxiv.org/abs/1911.12560
12. Liu, Z., Chen, Y., Yu, H., et al.: GTG-shapley: efficient and accurate participant contribution evaluation in federated learning. ACM Trans. Intell. Syst. Technol. **13**(4), 60:1–60:21 (2022)
13. Majeed, U., Hong, C.S.: FLchain: federated learning via MEC-enabled blockchain network. In: 2019 20th Asia-Pacific Network Operations and Management Symposium (APNOMS), pp. 1–4 (2019)
14. Naja, I., Markovic, M., Edwards, P., Cottrill, C.: A semantic framework to support AI system accountability and audit. In: Verborgh, R., et al. (eds.) ESWC 2021. LNCS, vol. 12731, pp. 160–176. Springer, Cham (2021). https://doi.org/10.1007/978-3-030-77385-4_10
15. Schad, J., Sambasivan, R., Woodward, C.: Arangopipe, a tool for machine learning meta-data management. Data Sci. **4**(2), 85–99 (2021)
16. Siebert, J., Joeckel, L., Heidrich, J., et al.: Construction of a quality model for machine learning systems. Softw. Qual. J. **2021**, 1–29 (2021)
17. Simon, G., Vincent, T.: A projected stochastic gradient algorithm for estimating shapley value applied in attribute importance. In: Holzinger, A., Kieseberg, P., Tjoa, A.M., Weippl, E. (eds.) CD-MAKE 2020. LNCS, vol. 12279, pp. 97–115. Springer, Cham (2020). https://doi.org/10.1007/978-3-030-57321-8_6
18. Souza, R., Azevedo, L., Lourenço, V., et al.: Provenance data in the machine learning lifecycle in computational science and engineering. In: 2019 IEEE/ACM Workflows in Support of Large-Scale Science (WORKS), pp. 1–10 (2019)
19. Wang, R.: Beyond accuracy: what data quality means to data consumers. J. Manage. Inf. Syst. **12**(4), 5–34 (1996)
20. Wang, T., Rausch, J., Zhang, C., Jia, R., Song, D.: A principled approach to data valuation for federated learning. In: Yang, Q., Fan, L., Yu, H. (eds.) Federated Learning. LNCS (LNAI), vol. 12500, pp. 153–167. Springer, Cham (2020). https://doi.org/10.1007/978-3-030-63076-8_11
21. Yang, Q., Liu, Y., Chen, T., Tong, Y.: Federated machine learning: concept and applications. ACM TIST **10**(2), 12:1–12:19 (2019)

Towards a Secure Peer-to-Peer Federated Learning Framework

Tim Piotrowski[✉] and Zoltán Nochta

Data-Centric Software Systems (DSS) Research Group,
Karlsruhe University of Applied Sciences - Institute of Applied Research,
Karlsruhe, Germany
{tim.piotrowski,zoltan.nochta}@h-ka.de

Abstract. Machine learning techniques are used in numerous applications to identify complex patterns and relationships in data. However, data of a single actor is often insufficient, as large amounts of data are required to train powerful machine learning models. One approach to tackle this problem is the federated training of models by multiple cooperating entities. However, the cooperation raises security and privacy concerns, especially if competitors are involved that do not want to share business critical training data with each other. We present a secure, privacy preserving, decentralized P2P Federated Learning framework to address these issues. The framework eliminates the need to establish a central trusted server for model training, which often represents a communication bottleneck or single point of failure. Various steps of data preprocessing, as well as the aggregation of individual models are carried out by means of Secure Multi-Party Computation to protect the data of training participants. We describe our experiments to demonstrate the basic feasibility of the working prototype and highlight open technical and methodological issues that we aim to address in the future.

Keywords: Security · Machine learning · Federated learning ·
Peer-to-peer · Private set intersection · Secure aggregation · Secure
multi-party computation

1 Introduction

Due to the ongoing trend to use machine learning (ML) to solve complex problems, new technology and approaches are constantly emerging. Federated Learning (FL) is such a recent advance in the field of ML. It allows multiple participants each having own data, to train a common model without exposing their local training data [7]. As no training data needs to be shared with other training participants, FL is considered to be a privacy-preserving improvement of machine learning.

Funded by the German Federal Ministry of Education and Research. Project name: KIWI, RefNr: 16KIS1142K.

However, recent research [2] shows that attacks based on the model output or model weights can extract information or even reverse engineer the underlying private training data. Therefore, FL alone is not sufficient to guarantee the security of training participants' sensitive data. Since an additional central server entity is responsible for the updates of the common model, the server needs to be trusted by all training participants in the first place. Although the server owner could apply the mentioned attacks to determine private data of all participants at once. Further, a central administration is at risk of becoming a bottleneck or single point of failure.

In the context of federated learning, each participant has to apply identical methods to prepare (e.g., normalize, clean, encode) its own training datasets, before the actual joint training process can start. To achieve this goal, the participants must exchange information, incl. Strings that occur in their tabular or categorical data, and also share different feature properties, such as min and max values, mean, standard deviation, etc. Obviously, not all participants are willing to reveal this information.

In this work, we propose a secure federated Peer-to-Peer (P2P) approach to protect the privacy of so called *"honest-but-curious"* (HBC) training participants, while providing them with greater autonomy and sovereignty regarding process control. Another objective, in addition to, data protection, is to reduce the risk of premature termination of model training due to failures of a central server. The paper focuses mainly on the following contributions: A prototype framework for P2P federated learning that supports multiple communication schemes. Integration of privacy preserving methods to secure local data from HBC peers using Secure Multi-Party Computation (SMPC) techniques during the training as well as the data preparation. Privacy-preserving preprocessing of local training datasets with the help of Private Set Intersection (PSI).

Subsequently, Sect. 2 introduces the problem statement and background of this research as well as a threat model including possible machine learning attack patterns. Afterwards, Sect. 3 deals with the conception of the framework and privacy-preserving methods to further enhance the security of federated learning. Section 4 summarizes our experiments based on a credit card fraud use case. In Sect. 5 related work is presented and, finally, Sect. 6 draws conclusions and gives an outlook for future work.

2 Problem Statement

Federated learning was originally proposed by Hard et al. [7] to execute the training of a Deep Neural Network (DNN) model on a large number of mobile devices. Hereby, a central server gathers model weights from connected devices, aggregates them and distributes the resulting model to the client devices. This procedure is repeated multiple times until the aggregated model converges. The model weight aggregation enables ML training based on multiple data sources, without data exchange or central data storage. Thus, federated learning partly preserves privacy.

Recently, attacks have been presented [11] to extract information about the underlying data or to even reconstruct [2, 17] the training data from known model weights. Considering those attacks, a central server represents a possible threat. As a third party that collects the weights, the central server could apply those attacks to obtain the private sensitive data of all clients. In this context, the server could also imitate a training with multiple participants to cheat a single participant. It could merely extract the participant's local data, add randomly generated weights to those of the participant and return the "resulting" model to him. Furthermore, a central server can be considered as a single point of failure in the training process. These challenges motivate the implementation of model training using a decentralized P2P approach. The approach is to entirely eliminate the central server, making model aggregation to a joint task of all training participants. Basically, the peers are willing to cooperate with each other to address common problems under the condition that no private information must be shared, as no mutual trust exists.

2.1 Underlying Threat Model

In our threat model, training participants are considered as untrustworthy. We assume that all participants are potential honest-but-curious (HBC) adversaries. Paverd et al. [13] define a honest-but-curious adversary as a legitimate participant in a communication protocol, who adheres to the defined protocol yet attempts to learn all possible information from legitimately received messages. Transferred to a FL use-case, it is a participant, who actively and honestly participates in the training, but possibly uses reconstruction or inference attacks to compute the otherwise unknown training data of other participants. To carry out such attacks, a HBC participant can use available information, such as the model architecture, configuration parameters, format of the training data, structure and mapping of the features as well as the model weight values that were computed by other participants.

Depending on the adversaries' intentions, the classification as "malicious adversary" might be even more suitable. The exploration of obtained information to blackmail or actively sabotage the daily business of other participants needs to be considered as threats. Peers that sabotage the training by injecting false data or only pretend to participate in the training to receive access to other participants' data and to the training results, are also commonly considered as malicious adversaries. In a FL scenario, HBC participants have different types of attacks at their disposal. Our current research focuses on white-box attacks. Hereby, the adversary has knowledge about the ML model architecture and the used parameters. Considering our threat model, this is the case, because the adversary is participating in the training protocol.

In particular, property inference attacks, reconstruction attacks and distribution attacks are of relevance for our research. Reconstruction attacks extract single data samples, underlying private training data, or the respective training labels for a given neural network model [15, 17].

Property inference attacks describe the prediction of dataset properties and relationships of the training data, that are not directly encoded as features or not integrated in the training process [15]. Other inference attacks try to recover sensitive features such as the distribution of training labels based on given outputs, labels and partial feature knowledge [15]. The gathered information can serve as a basis for further attacks [8,15].

2.2 Federated Preprocessing of Training and Test Data

The task of data preprocessing is often underestimated in literature, but in the context of FL it raises practical challenges regarding data privacy. Preprocessing refers to techniques of cleaning and transforming raw data to improve the quality of the training data and the resulting ML model. Standardization is one step within the preprocessing pipeline to map numerical feature values to values within a predefined range. Tabular datasets diverge between individual participants, since the features, e.g. strings, decimal values, are often not in a set interval. Thus, each local standardization process is unique and produces different values. To ensure identical standardisation on all local datasets, an exchange of feature information is needed between participants to determine metrics, such as min and max values, standard deviation, or mean value of a data set. Naturally, not all participants are willing to share this information. Converting categorical data into a processable numeric format proves to be a similar privacy-related problem in FL environments. The conversion usually requires a word dictionary. This dictionary assigns a unique number to each (string) entry. Error-free FL requires a dictionary implementation across all local data sets, so that all occurring categorical data items are uniquely identified system-wide. It is usually achieved by exchanging all strings that appear in local data sets. However, this contradicts the basic idea of privacy preserving FL as this leaks training data to the other participants. In conclusion, the federated preprocessing of training data can leak sensitive information and must be secured accordingly.

3   Concept of the Decentralized P2P Framework

In this chapter, we present the overall concept and underlying techniques of our decentralized P2P FL framework. The core idea of a federated P2P framework is to eliminate the need for a central server to run the model training. The framework will enable multiple (sometimes even competing) entities or institutions to join one or more peer groups in order to collaboratively train and evolve DNN models, which help participants solve common problems. In a commercial setting, a service provider, e.g. an IT company, might help organize and manage peer groups. The peer groups can be formed around, e.g., industry-specific, application cases that can benefit from the usage of jointly trained, and thus, powerful ML models. The orchestrator could for example offer a web-based access to join or leave specific peer groups on demand and allow peers to connect their local ML pipelines.

Furthermore, it can distribute initial (i.e., untrained) model architectures, offer training algorithms, suggest basic training parameters, such as batch sizes or learning rates, and provide participants with the proper software (libraries, tools) that are necessary to run decentralized federated learning. Note that, in general, the orchestrating entity will not actively participate in the actual model training processes, since it will usually not possess relevant training data. As there is no central server involved in the training anymore, the training participants must be made capable to run model training locally (based on local data) and also to collaboratively compute a joint model using a proper distributed protocol. While running the protocol each peer acts as both server and client. The respective protocol can support the creation and step-wise refinement of the joint model in a sequential or parallelized way. In an example sequential training process, the initial model is first trained by one of the peers (e.g., selected randomly) for a defined number of epochs. Afterwards, the model is passed on to the next participant, who trains further epochs. These steps are repeated until each participant has trained the model at least once and the model converges. Instead of averaging locally computed weights, the model is continuously trained by the participants. Note, that the first peer might generate significant bias, which cannot be compensated by the other participants later. Theoretically, reverse engineering of the underlying local training data should be increasingly difficult after multiple peers have trained on the model, since a curios participant cannot recognize specific updates made by a particular peer anymore. To better protect the local data of the first participant against attacks (e.g., performed by the second participant), some noise can be added to the transmitted model weights. Sequential approaches can be considered as rather slow, because the nodes must wait for each other. At the same time, they can improve the security of the process compared to server-based FL without using additional cryptographic methods, as none of the participants has information about model updates made by particular peer group members.

In a parallelized P2P training process, the participating peers simultaneously train their local model instances. The resulting model weights are exchanged after a defined number of epochs and can than be aggregated. The exchange of model weights between training participants can be implemented in various ways. Figure 1 shows a possible implementation of a parallel training protocol. The peer group, consisting of three participants, has already agreed in advance on the model architecture and basic configuration parameters. In the first step, raw training data, such as log files, are preprocessed locally, followed by a system-wide preprocessing, which peer group members carry out jointly (see details below). Based on the transformed data, local model training is initiated at each peer's premises. After completing a predefined number of local epochs, the computed weights can be exchanged between the participants in a broadcast manner, so that each training participant will know the locally computed weights of all other participants. Each participant then updates its local model by averaging its local weights and the weights it received from the others.

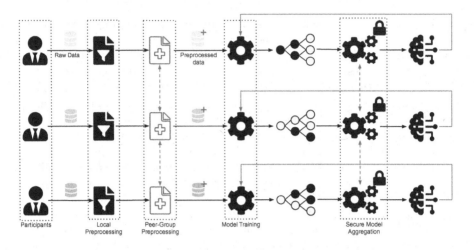

Fig. 1. Parallel P2P federated model training process

These training steps are repeated until the model converges, the quality metrics meet the requirements, or a predefined maximum number of epochs is reached. At the end, all participants are in possession of the same model. A more secure model aggregation would help hide actual weight values, and thus prevent potential leakage of underlying training data. Secure model aggregation can be realized by a number of different methods and algorithms. For example, it is possible to use SMPC methods or apply Differential Privacy [1]. A similar principle applies to the joint preprocessing of training data, where various security-related measures can be used in combination depending on the actual use case. In general, broadcasting the model weights leads to high communication load on each peer, which might cause bottlenecks in the system. With the help of all-reduce methods [12,21] the communication efforts can be minimized, as only smaller weight-chunks must be sent to specific peers instead of broadcasting all weights within the peer group.

3.1 Secure Model Aggregation

The ultimate goal of our decentralized P2P concept is to provide a privacy-preserving federated learning environment. Accordingly, additional methods are needed to enhance the above described federated learning process. As shown by our threat model, the exchange of model weights between participants represents a potential security vulnerability. Integrating SMPC techniques into the aggregation process could protect the local weights, and thus make reverse engineering of the training data highly difficult. SMPC provides different approaches for multiple participants to compute a function together without revealing their input values to the other participants. Currently, we consider the usage of two SMPC approaches in our framework.

In the approach presented in [19], a locally computed model weight x is randomly partitioned. The given peer generates n positive random numbers $r_1, r_2, ..., r_n$ for n participants including itself. These random numbers are then added up to a sum s_r. Using the random numbers and their sum, a unique exchange value $x_{i,j} = x * \frac{r_i}{s_r}$ for each participant i can be determined by participant j. Those exchange values are then send to the dedicated participant i while the one corresponding to participant j is kept as a secret. Each participant i then computes the sum $s_i = \sum_{j=0}^{j=n} x_{i,j}$ using the local computed exchange value and the values received from other participants. This value is then shared with the other participants, so that each peer can determine the average value μ_s. Finally, this mean value corresponds to the mean value μ_x of the actual weights. This enables, averaging without revealing the actual weights.

The second approach is a one-time pad (OTP) method by Bonawitz et al. [4]. First, the nodes form a hierarchy based on numbering or the like. Hereby, each node is assigned a hierarchical order v. Then the nodes randomly generate an OTP for each other network participant. Those OTPs are then exchanged between the nodes. Based on the OTPs, the participants form an intermediate sum y_i by adding the sum of all OTPs from nodes that are at higher hierarchy-level ($i < v$) to the local weight x, and correspondingly subtracting the sum of OTPs received from the lower ranked nodes ($i > v$). These intermediate results are then collected on a selected node, usually the hierarchically highest one. This node averages the sums and thus obtains the average of the local weights, which can be distributed back to the other nodes. Assuming three nodes a, b and c want to compute the average of their weights. Node a is selected as the highest and c as the lowest node in the hierarchy. Therefore, node a must subtract the OTPs of other participants from its local weight, while c must add all OTPs to its local weight. In contrast, b must add the OTP received from a and subtract the OTP of c. Then a collects the results to determine the final average and distribute it. The problem with this procedure is, that the participant on top of the hierarchy has some information advantage, since he calculates the average weight values prior to all other participants. It could be prevented by exchanging intermediate sums directly with all other nodes, which can then independently calculate the mean value. Beside the additional communication and computation costs, both methods are not resistant to node failures. The entire aggregation must be restarted as soon as one of the nodes drops out of the training prematurely.

3.2 Secure Preprocessing Tasks

SMPC procedures can also be applied to secure normalization during preprocessing. Assuming that the peer group decides to use the so-called z-score normalization to scale a given feature f_n. The z-score is calculated using the following formula:

$$z_n = \frac{x_n - \mu_n}{\sigma_n} \tag{1}$$

Here, x_n is a single value within the feature f_n of a local dataset, μ_n represents the mean and σ stands for the standard deviation of the feature.

In order to ensure identical normalization on all local datasets, both mean and standard deviation of the feature must be determined on a system level. For this purpose, the mean and the variance are determined for each local data set. Subsequently, the mean is weighted according to the size of the respective local data set I_n, so that local mean values of larger data sets receive more weighting. Thus, the system-wide average μ_g can be determined as follows:

$$\mu_g = \frac{\sum_{n=1}^{N} \mu_n * I_n}{\sum_{n=1}^{N} I_n} \tag{2}$$

The upper term represents the sum of all weighted local mean values and the lower term the size of the system-wide data set. Presuming that three participants with data sets of size 500, 600 and 700 are involved in the training, the lower term then corresponds to the value 1800.

For the determination of μ_g, sensitive data is exchanged, so it is advisable to use privacy preserving mechanisms such as SMPC at this point. However, it does not prevent each participant to receive the total number of training instances. Subtracting the size of the local datasets reveals the size of training data owned by other participants. Leaking this information does not seem to be a disadvantage, as peers can see in advance whether other partners have sufficient amounts of training data and thus the federated learning is lucrative. On the other hand, the knowledge could be used for attacks that we are not yet aware of or that will arise in the future.

Ad-hoc the addition of the local variances $v_1, ..., v_n$ is performed using the same protocol as in the mean calculation procedure. Identical to the mean value procedure, a division through the total number of training data is needed. The obtained system-wide variance has to be finally rooted to receive the standard deviation σ_g. This results in the following formula for a federated standard deviation:

$$\sigma_g = \sqrt{\frac{\sum_{n=1}^{N} \sigma_n^2}{\sum_{n=1}^{N} I_n}} \tag{3}$$

Providing secure categorical data conversion in a federated learning environment proves to be another important topic. As part of the preprocessing, categorical data is converted into a processable format. In order to ensure a unique representation and identification of the strings, all occurring unique strings within a given feature are collected in a dictionary. Based on the dictionary, the words are then numbered consecutively. To guarantee unique identification in a federated environment, this dictionary must be created on a peer-group level. Normally, it would require the disclosure of private local data instances. This directly contradicts our vision of a secure P2P federation. Therefore, we want to integrate PSI [6] into the preprocessing. PSI is a cryptographic technique that allows two parties to compute the intersection of their sets without revealing data except the intersection. Based on the intersection, the participants agree on unique numbers to ensure a clear identification and unique encoding of data items.

Subsequently, the remaining words in the local dictionaries can be incrementally assigned to numbers. Suppose, participant P_1 possesses the set of strings $S_1 = \{Dog, Cat, Mouse\}$ and participant P_2 has $S_2 = \{Cat, Elephant, Snake\}$. Using PSI, they compute the intersection $S_1 \cap S_2 = \{Cat\}$. Subsequently, both participants agree to encode "Cat" as 1. Then participant P_1 creates her dictionary $D_1 = \{Dog = 0, Cat = 1, Mouse = 2\}$ and informs P_2 about the highest number she issued. Based on this, P_2 creates the following dictionary $D_2 = \{Cat = 1, Elephant = 3, Snake = 4\}$. As a result, a unique identification and encoding of strings is achieved in the system. Microsoft provides the APSI (Asymmetric PSI)[1] library to implement PSI. The library provides a PSI functionality for asymmetric sets. This will be integrated into the framework in the course of our research to see whether it could provide an solution to the problem.

4 Experiments

In order to prove the applicability of our concepts, several experiments were conducted. As example scenario the detection of illicit credit card transactions was chosen: Several banks want to jointly train a fraud detection model, since fraudulent transactions rarely occur on a large scale. Obviously, none of the banks wants to disclose training data, i.e. its credit card transaction logs, to its competitors.

4.1 DNN Architecture and Example Dataset

To tackle credit card fraud, we train a deep neural network. It consists of two main parts. The first part, consisting of three dense layers, classifies the current transaction on the basis of all transactions in the training data. The second part uses a sliding window approach on the transaction history of the given credit card number of the examined transaction. It consists of a Long Short-Term Memory (LSTM) layer and two additional dense layers. The outputs of both parts are finally concatenated to conclude a final classification statement using an output layer. The model has been trained on the Simulated Credit Card Transactions dataset[2]. It was generated using Sparkov Data Generation[3] in combination with a pre-defined lists of imaginary merchants, customers and transaction categories. The dataset contains approximately 1.85 million simulated credit card transactions of 1000 customers in the USA between 01-01-2019 and 31-12-2020. The experiments covered the features credit card number, merchant, amount spent, job, timestamp, latdif and longdif, the latter describing the difference between the customer's and the merchant's location. Similar to real world cases, fraudulent transactions occur rather rarely in this dataset. Therefore, we decided to sub-sample licit transactions, so that the difference between the categories is significantly reduced.

---

[1] https://github.com/microsoft/APSI.
[2] https://www.kaggle.com/kartik2112/fraud-detection.
[3] https://github.com/namebrandon/Sparkov_Data_Generation.

4.2 Procedure and Evaluation

In the first step, the training dataset was divided into four approximately identically sized parts to represent the data of four distinct banks of similar size. Using these partial datasets as input we ran the training of local models of each simulated bank for 100 epochs. In the next step, these banks built a peer-group and trained together a joint model using our prototype framework. Based on F1-score the quality of the resulting models is evaluated. Since there is still an imbalance between the two classes, fraud and legitimate transaction, despite preprocessing, e.g., resampling, we calculate the F1-score for each class separately, and average it (macro F1-Score) afterwards. As expected, the federated training process led to a model of higher F1-scores. While individual local training achieved an F1 in the range of 83–86%, the combination helped reach an F1 score of 93%. This underpins the basic functionality of our P2P approach and prototype. In addition, we performed a run-time comparison between parallel P2P training without SMPC and with SMPC [19]. For this purpose, a computer with an Intel i5-10310U processor and 16 GB RAM was used. Respectively the unsecured approach takes approximately 28 min while the latter takes 32 min. Thus, the training of the same model is prolonged by almost 4 min using secure aggregation. Up to now, the training takes place on a single computer via containers, so a fair run-time comparison between a local training and a truly remote networked peer-group training was not yet ensured.

To demonstrate the necessity and effectiveness of SMPC procedures explained earlier, we attempted to perform an inference and label prediction attack on the credit card dataset. Hence, we extended and adapted the available Update Leaks code by Ahmed Salem et al. [17] to fit our use case. Hereby, the output differences of a given model are used to train the adversaries models. These differences are generated by the model predicting the same data several times after continuous training updates based on small datasets. The observed differences are used to extract information about the respective update dataset. In order to keep the experiments as similar as possible to our threat model, we only use the training and test data available to a single participant to train the attack models. Label prediction proved to be less successful, due to the uneven distribution of the dataset as non-fraud transactions are represented four times more than fraudulent transactions. This attack attempts to predict a probability distribution of the labels that occur in the update, and tries to predict the most frequently occurring label. In our dataset, however, this is almost always the label representing non-fraud transactions. Using smaller updates would prevent this problem. However, the label attack would then not be applicable in a real scenario, as updates are based on a whole epoch and thus tend to be larger. As an alternative to the model developed by Ahmed et al., we also created our own attack inference model. Instead of the differences of the final output, this model uses only the output difference of the first neural network component explained earlier. We conducted the experiments with several different update set sizes and hyper-parameters, e.g., learning rate and batch size. Thereby, the Mean Squared Error loss (MSE) was used to evaluate the similarity between the original and the data generated by the inference model. The best model could only achieve a loss of 0.59. Examination of the generated data also showed that the model was not able to approximate the update set data. Thus, in the current state of our research, we could not generate an attack that would predict underlying data information with a high probability, to justify the essential demand for SMPC measures in a decentralized FL setting.

5   Related Work

Considering that training based on multiple data sources and thus more diverse training data is beneficial, federated learning is a well researched topic in science [7,10,14]. As the central server entity proves to be a bottleneck for scalability [9] and a single point of failure, research activities on decentralization and secure federation are emerging.

BrainTorrent [16] is the concept of a federated P2P system. Hereby, peers compute their local model weights and independently request updates from other peers. Peers that have newer model versions send their weights on request. Based on those weights, the peers can average a global model using own and received local weights. Thus, the presented method represents an asynchronous approach, which should result in a generally faster runtime of the individual nodes. In comparison, our approach uses a synchronous communication pattern that accepts a longer runtime in order to avoid so-called *deprecated updates*, which occur when one of the participants has hardware that is too slow and so the discrepancy between the epochs of the fastest and the slowest node needs to be considered. Bellet et al. [3] introduce a fully decentralized and asynchronous algorithm for P2P machine learning as well. In addition, the authors secure the training process by applying differential privacy to train personalized models. Basically, the usage of differential privacy represents an alternative technique to protect local training data. It could also be used in combination with SMPC methods as well.

Shayan et al. [18] present a secure decentralized FL framework called Biscotti. Biscotti uses a blockchain to communicate and store model weights. The underlying threat model deals with malicious adversaries. Their intention is to negatively impact the training results by poisoning. In contrast, in our framework we assume less malicious, i.e., HBC participants. Biscotti prevents poisoning attacks by verifying the contributions of training participants to the common model. This verification method is mainly based on the Byzantine tolerant gradient descent. In addition, a noising protocol is used to protect local SGD updates against adversaries' attacks.

Wittkopp et al. [20] introduce a decentralized learning approaches that uses a teacher and student model principle. Instead of exchanging gradients or weights, the student models are trained on the output of their teachers and combined with synthetically generated auxiliary samples. In a decentralized system each node acts therefore as teacher and student at the same time.

Li Chou et al. [5] propose a less centralized approach to implement federated learning. Thereby, multiple participants are grouped in smaller peer-to-peer groups to communicate with each other. Each peer-group uses an all-reduce method to calculate a group model before sending it to the central server for aggregation. This hybrid model reduces the communication load on the central server without eliminating it. At the same time, it could reduce the attack accuracy of the server too, since the server does not longer receive individual models weights of peers.

6   Conclusion and Future Work

We presented our vision of a framework for P2P federated learning, that enables collaborating business entities to jointly generate and evolve machine learning models, while preventing private data leakage. As training participants independently carry out every computational task, incl. training initialization, model training, model aggregation, etc., there is no need to involve any other third party system or service provider in the process. Improved data security is ensured by incorporating SMPC methodology during the preprocessing of training data as well as during the aggregation of locally computed models. Experiments on the real live scenario of credit card fraud using a synthetic dataset proved that our prototype works as presumed and can already be used to train in a P2P federated fashion. In particular, the inclusion of SMPC does not seem to have a particularly strong impact on the overall training duration. Since the experiments were performed on a single computer, a future test using a cluster is desirable. Under these circumstances the secret sharing and the P2P training should be considerably faster. Preferable using real rather than synthetic data. Although it remains to be seen, whether SMPC can actually protect against various attacks based on weights. Based on the results so far, this could not be clearly determined. Future experiments on this topic will research different attacks and additional security mechanisms. Especially in the communication scheme, various optimizations may still possible to speed up the training or to minimize the communication effort. In this context distributed learning provides various inspirations. Furthermore, conversion of categorical data on a system wide level could potentially be realized using PSI to prevent additional data leakage. Besides PSI and z-score normalisation other preprocessing operations like min-max normalization should be integrated into the framework. Moreover, future research envisages the inclusion of other machine learning algorithms, such as decision trees in the P2P framework in addition to neural networks.

References

1. Abadi, M., et al.: Deep learning with differential privacy. In: Proceedings of the 2016 ACM SIGSAC Conference on Computer and Communications Security, pp. 308–318 (2016)
2. Aïvodji, U., Gambs, S., Ther, T.: GAMIN: an adversarial approach to black-box model inversion. CoRR abs/1909.11835 (2019)
3. Bellet, A., Guerraoui, R., Taziki, M., Tommasi, M.: Personalized and private peer-to-peer machine learning. In: AISTATS, vol. 84, pp. 473–481. PMLR (2018)
4. Bonawitz, K., et al., V.I.: Practical secure aggregation for privacy-preserving machine learning. In: Thuraisingham, B.M., et al., D.E. (eds.) Proceedings of the 2017 ACM SIGSAC Conference on Computer and Communications Security, CCS, pp. 1175–1191. ACM (2017)

5. Chou, L., Liu, Z., Wang, Z., Shrivastava, A.: Efficient and less centralized federated learning. In: Oliver, N., Pérez-Cruz, F., Kramer, S., Read, J., Lozano, J.A. (eds.) ECML PKDD 2021. LNCS, vol. 12975, pp. 772–787. Springer, Cham (2021). https://doi.org/10.1007/978-3-030-86486-6_47

6. Cong, K., et al.: Labeled psi from homomorphic encryption with reduced computation and communication. Cryptology ePrint Archive, Report 2021/1116 (2021). https://ia.cr/2021/1116

7. Hard, A., et al.: Federated learning for mobile keyboard prediction. CoRR abs/1811.03604 (2018)

8. He, Z., Zhang, T., Lee, R.B.: Model inversion attacks against collaborative inference. In: Proceedings of the 35th Annual Computer Security Applications Conference, pp. 148–162. ACSAC 2019, Association for Computing Machinery, New York, NY, USA (2019). https://doi.org/10.1145/3359789.3359824

9. Kairouz, P., McMahan, H.B., Avent, B., Bellet, A., Bennis, M., et al.: Advances and open problems in federated learning. CoRR abs/1912.04977 (2019). http://arxiv.org/abs/1912.04977

10. Konečný, J., McMahan, H.B., Yu, F.X., Richtarik, P., Suresh, A.T., Bacon, D.: Federated learning: strategies for improving communication efficiency. In: NIPS Workshop on Private Multi-Party Machine Learning (2016)

11. Melis, L., Song, C., Cristofaro, E.D., Shmatikov, V.: Inference attacks against collaborative learning. CoRR abs/1805.04049 (2018). http://arxiv.org/abs/1805.04049

12. Patarasuk, P., Yuan, X.: Bandwidth optimal all-reduce algorithms for clusters of workstations. J. Parallel Distrib. Comput. **69**(2), 117–124 (2009). https://doi.org/10.1016/j.jpdc.2008.09.002

13. Paverd, A.J., Martin, A.C.: Modelling and automatically analysing privacy properties for honest-but-curious adversaries (2014)

14. Reddi, S.J., et al.: Adaptive federated optimization. In: International Conference on Learning Representations (2021)

15. Rigaki, M., Garcia, S.: A survey of privacy attacks in machine learning (2021)

16. Roy, A.G., Siddiqui, S., Pölsterl, S., Navab, N., Wachinger, C.: BrainTorrent: a peer-to-peer environment for decentralized federated learning. CoRR abs/1905.06731 (2019)

17. Salem, A., Bhattacharya, A., Backes, M., Fritz, M., Zhang, Y.: Updates-leak: data set inference and reconstruction attacks in online learning. In: 29th USENIX Security Symposium (USENIX Security 20), pp. 1291–1308. USENIX Association (2020), https://www.usenix.org/conference/usenixsecurity20/presentation/salem

18. Shayan, M., Fung, C., Yoon, C.J.M., Beschastnikh, I.: Biscotti: a ledger for private and secure peer-to-peer machine learning. CoRR abs/1811.09904 (2018). http://arxiv.org/abs/1811.09904

19. Wink, T., Nochta, Z.: An approach for peer-to-peer federated learning. In: Proceedings of 51st Annual IEEE/IFIP International Conference on Dependable Systems and Networks Workshops (DSN-W) (2021)

20. Wittkopp, T., Acker, A.: Decentralized federated learning preserves model and data privacy. In: Hacid, H., et al. (eds.) ICSOC 2020. LNCS, vol. 12632, pp. 176–187. Springer, Cham (2021). https://doi.org/10.1007/978-3-030-76352-7_20

21. Zhao, H., Canny, J.F.: Sparse allreduce: efficient scalable communication for power-law data. CoRR abs/1312.3020 (2013). http://arxiv.org/abs/1312.3020

MIDA: Micro-flow Independent Detection of DDoS Attacks with CNNs

Samuel Kopmann[1]([✉]), Hauke Heseding[1,2], and Martina Zitterbart[1,2]

[1] Institute of Telematics, Karlsruhe Institute of Technology, Karlsruhe, Germany
{samuel.kopmann,hauke.heseding,martina.zitterbart}@kit.edu
[2] KASTEL - Security Research Labs, Karlsruhe, Germany

Abstract. This work proposes the novel approach MIDA for detecting volumetric *Distributed Denial of Service* (DDoS) attacks. To avoid processing individual micro-flows during ongoing high-volume attacks, an efficient traffic aggregation scheme preserving detection-relevant traffic characteristics is introduced. To this end, traffic is aggregated into a compact, two-dimensional image representation that facilitates classification with *Convolutional Neural Networks* (CNNs). The feasibility of the attack detection is evaluated using different data sets, including the CIC-IDS2017 and synthesized data sets. In addition, MIDA includes a CNN based approach to derive network filter rules for attack mitigation. In essence, the approach applies well-studied concepts from the area of computer vision (image classification and segmentation) to realize DDoS attack detection and mitigation on traffic aggregates.

Keywords: Machine learning · Intrusion detection system · DDoS · CNN · Sliding window · CIC-IDS 2017 · Image classification

1 Introduction

Protecting network infrastructures against volumetric DDoS attacks remains a challenging task, due to increasing line speeds and an ever-growing amount of connected devices on the Internet. *Machine Learning* (ML) offers a promising approach for anomaly detection in network traffic. Recent approaches [4,9,15] analyze traffic on the granularity of micro-flows, which are identified by the following five-tuple: source IP-address, destination IP-address, source port, destination port and the transport protocol. Such fine-granular traffic processing is problematic in the context of DDoS attacks, since attackers can potentially create an arbitrary amount of micro-flows, e.g., by spoofing IP-addresses. This introduces an additional vulnerability, since state-keeping for individual flows can exhaust memory and processing resources, effectively turning the detection system into the primary bottleneck in a volumetric DDoS scenario. To avoid fine-grained state-keeping of individual flows, the proposed approach uses aggregated traffic characteristics. To aggregate network traffic at line speed, multiple packet fields, e.g., IP-addresses and port numbers, need to be matched as fast

C. Zirpins et al. (Eds.): ESOCC 2022 Workshops, CCIS 1617, pp. 32–43, 2022.
https://doi.org/10.1007/978-3-031-23298-5_3

as possible. This can be achieved by using *ternary content-addressable memory* (TCAM) [16]. With TCAM multi-field classification can be performed within a single clock cycle. However, TCAM capacity is limited by high costs and high energy consumption. Therefore, a sustainable aggregation scheme should only need a very limited amount of TCAM. Care must be taken to retain detection-relevant information when performing traffic aggregation, since aggregation typically leads to loss of information.

This paper presents MIDA, a novel aggregation approach coping with increasing volumes of traffic data, while still keeping the need for TCAM space low. In addition to the efficient aggregation scheme, an attack detection and mitigation system based on CNNs is proposed. CNNs have been successful over the last decades considering computer vision tasks like image classification [3,6,7]. With the aggregation scheme introduced in this work, network attack detection can be accomplished through image classification, building a bridge from the area of computer vision to the area of DDoS attack detection and mitigation. All CNNs in this work are trained in a supervisory manner. I.e., prior to deployment the detection models are trained offline based on available data sets. The proposed system is considered to be deployed in a *software-defined network* (SDN), as TCAM is typically available in SDN-switches and aggregation rules can be implemented for fast multi-field classification.

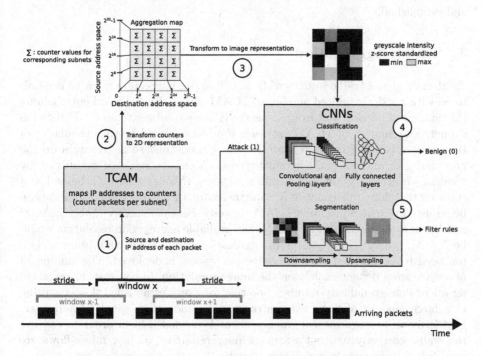

Fig. 1. Illustration of the MIDA workflow and its components

2   MIDA in a Nutshell

Architecture and workflow of MIDA are illustrated in Fig. 1 and include the following five different components: 1) sliding window 2) TCAM aggregation 3) image transformation 4) CNN classification, and 5) image segmentation. The traffic is divided by a time-based sliding window (1) and aggregated in two dimensions: the source and destination IP address space. The source and destination address spaces are divided into N disjoint subnets of equal size. For each combination of source and destination IP subnets, an entry is programmed into TCAM, to monitor the number of packets sent between the subnets (2) for every window. Consequently, the number of TCAM entries is bounded by the subnet resolution. The packet count in a given time interval (window size) is referred to as traffic intensity. The traffic intensities are fetched and reset periodically, depending on the stride of the sliding window, and are transformed into a two-dimensional array representing traffic intensities between source and destination subnets. Finally, the aggregation map is transformed to an image representation (3) by applying z-score standardization. The image is subsequently used for traffic classification based on CNNs (4), resulting in a binary decision indicating whether an attack is detected or not. If an attack is detected, image segmentation (pixel-to-pixel mapping) is performed afterwards (5) to determine the subnets containing DDoS traffic. Corresponding network filter rules can then be derived and established.

3   Traffic Aggregation

To identify attack traffic sources while avoiding per-flow context, traffic is monitored with a strictly limited number of TCAM entries. Each TCAM entry counts the number of packets sent from a specific IP source subnet to an IP destination subnet. The number of TCAM entries is a-priori bounded by the granularity of IP subnets, avoiding complex state-keeping. In contrast to aggregation on the granularity of micro-flows, where attackers can enforce resource exhaustion by creating an arbitrary amount of different flows, this aggregation scheme has a constant matching rule count of N^2. Furthermore, the aggregation resolution can be adjusted to match available TCAM capacity. For instance, let R_a be the total number of available entries in TCAM, the available aggregation resolution would be $N_a \cdot N_a$, where $N_a = \lfloor \sqrt{R_a} \rfloor$. All aggregation rules are known a priori and do not need to be changed once the detection system is deployed. The amount of necessary rules depends solely on the image resolution. In contrast, aggregation on micro-flow granularity requires one rule for every established flow, resulting in a large amount of flows when attackers are allowed to spoof IP addresses. Furthermore, aggregation rule management is needed [14], in order to capture the traffic correctly and not waste memory resources, as new micro-flows are established permanently and others vanish.

Sliding Window

The advantage of using a sliding window is to avoid outdated monitoring information in the detection process, yet to achieve sufficient stability of monitoring information. In addition, consecutive windows can be calculated efficiently because they contain shared values due to their overlap in time. The incoming data stream is divided by a sliding window over time for further processing. The arrival time of each packet determines the corresponding window.

For the application of a sliding window two parameters, w_d and w_s, are defined, where w_d represents the size of the sliding window and w_s its stride. The size is the duration of the aggregation time interval, which is the time span from the beginning of the window until its end. Too large windows risk the use of out-dated information in the detection process, whereas too small windows do not provide sufficient information for reliable classification. The stride is the offset in time between the start of two consecutive windows. The classification frequency depends on the stride. The smaller the stride is, the faster a potential attack can be detected and countermeasures be established.

4 Classification with CNNs

CNNs are used in this work to perform a binary classification. Standardized aggregation maps serve as input images and the classification result indicates whether attack traffic is contained in the input image or not. Current state-of-the-art CNN models, like *VGG16* [13], can be trained to classify high resolution images given sets of thousands of different classes [2]. Those models contain several million trainable parameters. Because all images in this work have a resolution of 32×32 and there are only two different classes, a custom lightweight model is used for classification. It contains 26.645 trainable parameters. All layers use the *Rectified Linear Unit* activation function, except the last layer, which uses the *sigmoid* activation function. Table 1 contains a summary of the used classification model. For further evaluations with images having higher resolutions than 32×32, larger models like *VGG16* are considered for classification.

Filter Rules through Image Segmentation

In addition to attack detection, generated traffic aggregation maps can be used to determine filter rules to discard attack traffic. This is accomplished by using another technique from the area of computer vision, namely semantic image segmentation [10]. When segmenting an image semantically, the input image is transformed to an equally sized output image. The performed transformation is a pixel-wise classification resulting in a pixel-to-pixel mapping. The image segmentation training is also performed in a supervisory manner. For every input image the respective target image needs to be known. To determine rules for traffic filtering, each pixel indicates whether address spaces contain attack traffic or benign traffic exclusively after segmentation. The input images are derived from

Table 1. Architecture of the CNN classification model

CNN												
Input (32x32)	Convolution (3x3, 16)	Convolution (3x3, 16)	MaxPooling (2x2)	Dropout (0.1)	Convolution (3x3, 16)	Convolution (3x3, 16)	MaxPooling (2x2)	Dropout (0.1)	Flatten	Dense (32)	Dense (2)	Dense (1)

traffic aggregation maps. Figure 2 illustrates the input, output and the target of a segmentation during the training with the synthesized data set. Target image creation requires a more detailed label assignment, because a label needs to be assigned to every pair of subnets of the aggregation map instead of assigning a single label for the whole aggregation map. Once a traffic aggregation map is segmented, network filter rules can be derived by iterating over all pixels of the output image. For every pixel of the image that is assigned the DDoS label, the respective pair of subnets and therefore the part of the address space containing attack traffic can be determined. This allows establishing corresponding filter rules in TCAM. Packets that match those filter rules are then dropped. In contrast to the traffic aggregation, filter rules do not need to be determined at line speed (although their fast computation is desirable). In contrast to the binary classification, the filter rule quality depends on the resolution of the traffic aggregation maps, since higher image resolutions can yield more precise filter rules. The model for image segmentation contains 471.568 trainable parameters. It utilizes dropout layers, as well as skip connections like in the *U-Net* architecture [12].

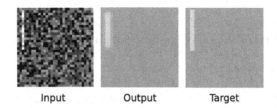

Input   Output   Target

Fig. 2. Image segmentation three-tuple (input, output, target) of a synthesized data set

5   Data Sets

For the training of CNN models, two different data sets are utilized: (a) the CIC-IDS2017 data set with real-world traffic and (b) synthesized aggregation maps. All data sets need to contain aggregation maps with the corresponding labels, which is not the case for the CIC-IDS2017 data set initially. In addition, the data sets for image segmentation training also contain target images.

Labeling Data. To train the CNNs in a supervisory manner, an aggregation map is created for every stride and a corresponding label (DDoS, Benign) is assigned based on a pre-defined threshold T_p as follows: if the number of attack packets is at least T_p within the time frame of a sliding window, the label "DDoS" is assigned to the stride, otherwise the label "Benign" is assigned. We use $T_p = 1$ for the CIC-IDS2017 data set. For other data and parameter sets, this threshold value can be adjusted, as lower threshold values make the detection of an attack harder or almost impossible, e.g., the detection of an attack in a window containing tens of thousands of legitimate packets but only one attack packet. Therefore, the parameter represents a sensitivity regulator, providing the possibility to adjust the detection system's tolerance against attack traffic.

CIC-IDS2017. The CIC-IDS2017 data set [1] is provided by the *Canadian Institute for Cybersecurity* (CIC) and the *University of New Brunswick* (UNB). It contains a broad variety of different attacks, captured at five different days. We focus on the Friday afternoon dataset, containing a DDoS attack. The data provides labels on micro-flow granularity. As the CNN training requires labeled aggregation maps, the flow-labels need to be transferred to the corresponding packets (by matching the five-tuple and the time stamps). But the labels of the aggregated flows cannot be applied to the packets without problems, such as ambiguous flow identifiers and too coarse time stamps, which are also already mentioned by Liang et al. [9]. The fact, that there is no packet to flow mapping publicly available, implies that the majority of intrusion detection systems, which use the CIC-IDS2017 data set for training, focuses on micro-flow classification.

The attack occurs during a limited time frame between 3:56 pm and 4:16 pm. Figure 3 illustrates the traffic intensity of Benign and DDoS traffic, represented by the number of packets received within a window. The distinction between attack and benign traffic uses a window of size and stride $w_s = w_d = 1$ min. It shows that windows containing attack traffic are not difficult to detect for this particular data set when inspecting the intensity feature. The attack detection can be performed on the basis of a constant packet-count threshold, as the attack traffic intensity is about five times larger than the Benign background traffic and the attack pattern is not developing during the attack, which can be classified as *constant rate* attack [11].

To model more complex attack traffic patterns, an additional synthesized data set is employed, which will be made publicly available.

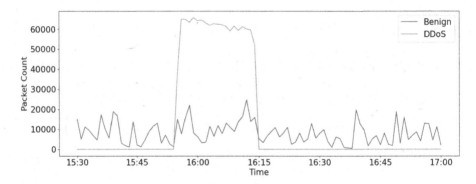

Fig. 3. CIC-IDS2017 (friday afternoon) traffic intensity over time, measured in one minute time intervals

Synthesized Data. The synthesized data directly models traffic intensity aggregation maps. Those aggregation maps either belong to the class *DDoS* or *Benign*. Each aggregation map models aggregated data for background traffic and attack traffic. A Benign aggregation map does only consist of background traffic. DDoS aggregation maps contain the additional attack traffic component, that models an attack from a randomly selected, continuous half of the source address space. The attack has a single target subnet in the destination address space. All aggregation maps have a resolution of $N = 32$ and floating-point pixel values representing traffic intensity (number of packets sent between a source and destination IP subnet within the sliding window). Benign traffic is assumed to be present in every pixel of the aggregation map and is randomly drawn from a uniform distribution over the interval $[90.0, 110.0]$. All aggregation maps are standardized using the *z-score normalization* before the training process begins. Further, attack traffic targets a single victim in the destination address space and its intensity is a fixed fraction of the background intensity (pixel-wise calculation). Pixel values in the final aggregation map represent the sum of its corresponding background and attack traffic intensity. Figure 4 illustrates the same DDoS attack (regarding the address space) multiple times, but with different intensities. For illustration purposes, all aggregation maps displayed in figures have been linearly scaled to the interval $[0, 255]$, representing grey-scale images. Synthesized aggregation maps do not seek to resemble authentic traffic distributions, but serve to evaluate detection capabilities in more complex scenarios (in comparison to the CIC-IDS2017 data set). To evaluate the effectiveness of the proposed approach, namely the lowest detectable attack intensity, twelve data sets with different attack intensities (see Fig. 4) have been created, each containing 50k Benign and 50k DDoS aggregation maps. In contrast to low intensity attacks, the attack traffic intensity of the CIC-IDS2017 data is about 5 times larger than the background traffic (see Fig. 3), which corresponds to the 500% DDoS example in Fig. 4.

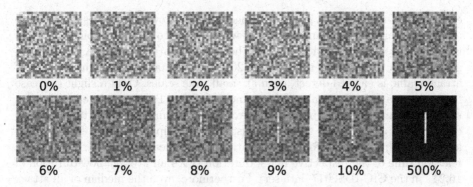

Fig. 4. DDoS aggregation maps of synthesized data sets for different attack intensities

6 Performance Results

The attack detection performance of the approach is evaluated on both the CIC-IDS2017 and the synthesized data sets regarding different metrics, e.g., False Positives and False Negatives. A subnet resolution of $N = 32$ is used. Each data set is split into the training set (80% of the data) and the test set (20% of the data). The training set is only used for the training process. Metrics are exclusively derived from the test set, which the CNN model does not process during training. In the context of this work, the positive label corresponds to the *DDoS* class and the negative label to the *Benign* class. Furthermore, P represents the number of *DDoS* samples in a data set and N the number of all *Benign* samples. *True Positives* (TP) and *True Negatives* (TN) are the amount of samples in a classified data set that have been assigned the correct label by the ML-model. *False Positives* (FP) and *False Negatives* (FN) denote the samples that were falsely classified as *DDoS* traffic and *Benign* traffic, respectively. Accuracy (1), precision (2), and recall (3) are defined as follows:

$$acc = \frac{TP + TN}{P + N} \quad (1) \quad pre = \frac{TP}{TP + FP} \quad (2) \quad rec = \frac{TP}{TP + FN} \quad (3)$$

Only balanced data sets are used for evaluation. Therefore, the CIC-IDS2017 data is cropped at the start and the end, resulting in the same amount of time with and without an ongoing attack (about 20 min each).

Detection Performance of the CIC-IDS2017 Data Set

Table 2 summarizes the detection accuracy of the trained model based on different window sizes and strides. Intuitively, a larger window size should yield higher accuracy, since larger windows contain more aggregated information. On the other hand larger windows can contain more information that is out-dated and therefore influence the classification result negatively, e.g., if the start or the end of an occurring attack is in a classified window. However, the results indicate almost the same performance for every window size to stride combination. This is due to the very imbalanced relation between the attack traffic and the background traffic intensity in the CIC-IDS2017 data set, as such a high intensity of attack traffic is easy to detect, even at small time scales. Only a slight decrease in the accuracy is detectable for a window of size 1 s. Despite reduced accuracy, achieving a reaction time (time from the beginning of an attack until its detection) of a fraction of a second constitutes an improvement over flow-based approaches that often perform classification on completed flows [8], resulting in a reaction time of the respective flows' duration (with an average flow duration of 16.24 s in the CIC-IDS2017 data set). Furthermore, even the median of all attack flows' duration is 1.7 s, while the flow duration represents the worst case reaction time of approaches that require complete flow context of the training data set for the classification. Regarding performance, the trade-off between window size and stride must be considered, since lower strides can facilitate detection on small time scales but also require a greater investment of computational resources.

Table 2. Achieved accuracy for different parameter sets of w_s and w_d regarding the CIC-IDS2017 data set after 200 epochs

Stride	Size					
	1 s	5 s	10 s	20 s	40 s	60 s
5%	0.9786	0.9963	0.9977	1	0.9964	1
10%	0.9758	0.9986	0.9973	1	0.9927	1
20%	0.9723	0.9954	0.9982	0.9891	0.9927	1

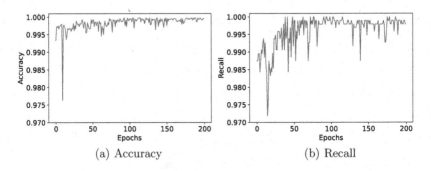

(a) Accuracy   (b) Recall

Fig. 5. Accuracy and recall for 5 s window and 0.25 s stride

Figure 5 exemplarily (for $w_d = 5$ s and $w_s = 5\%, w_d = 0.25$ s) shows the development of the achieved accuracy and recall on the CIC-IDS2017 test set during the training process (200 epochs). The maximum is already achieved after 50 epochs, which infers that the learning problem is not difficult and a resolution of $N = 32$ is sufficient to detect the contained attack traffic pattern.

Aggregating on the granularity of micro-flows, also achieves an accuracy of 100%, but goes along with a significantly larger memory overhead (memory space per flow). The application of the proposed approach with a resolution of $N = 32$ requires 1024 matching rules established in TCAM, independent of the micro-flow count. In contrast, the maximum of active micro-flows in the CIC-IDS2017 data set is 3172 considering a 10 s observation interval. However, the data set comprises only 20 different machines. In scenarios with a significantly larger number of attack sources (typical for DDoS attacks), memory savings due to aggregation become more pronounced.

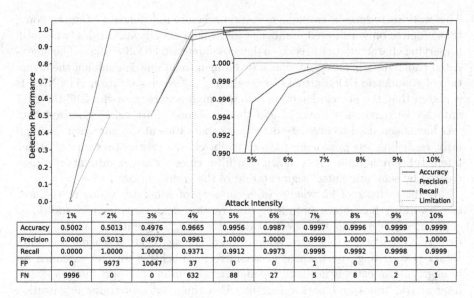

	1%	2%	3%	4%	5%	6%	7%	8%	9%	10%
Accuracy	0.5002	0.5013	0.4976	0.9665	0.9956	0.9987	0.9997	0.9996	0.9999	0.9999
Precision	0.0000	0.5013	0.4976	0.9961	1.0000	1.0000	0.9999	1.0000	1.0000	1.0000
Recall	0.0000	1.0000	1.0000	0.9371	0.9912	0.9973	0.9995	0.9992	0.9998	0.9999
FP	0	9973	10047	37	0	0	1	0	0	0
FN	9996	0	0	632	88	27	5	8	2	1

Fig. 6. Detection performance depending on the attack intensity in percent (Color figure online)

Detection Performance on Synthesized Aggregation Maps

Figure 6 illustrates the achieved performance of the CNN model on the synthesized aggregation maps, containing 20k samples of the corresponding data. The higher the attack intensity is compared to the background traffic, the better is the detection performance regarding all of the given metrics. Intuitively, with increased attack intensity the detection metrics should improve, since attack characteristics become more evident. This assumption corresponds to the evaluation metrics obtained when classifying synthesized aggregation maps with the CNN-based approach as outlined in Fig. 6. If the attack intensity is zero (no attack traffic at all), the model cannot become better than guessing, as Benign and DDoS samples do not differ from each other. Furthermore, the results show that the tested model can already detect an occurring attack if the attack intensity is only four percent of the background intensity. This threshold is illustrated by the vertical red line.

Segmentation Performance of Synthesized Aggregation Maps

The training results of the image segmentation trained on synthesized data is illustrated in Fig. 2. The segmentation achieves a high accuracy within the first few epochs, reaching 99%. The first two images in Fig. 2 show an example segmentation of an image that was captured during the training process, where the colors green and cyan represent the classes DDoS and Benign.

7 Conclusion and Future Work

This work introduces a traffic aggregation scheme, independent of micro-flows, that requires only a limited number of multi-field classification rules, while still preserving characteristics needed to detect volumetric DDoS attacks. The aggregated traffic data is represented as a two-dimensional image, enabling the detection of volumetric DDoS attacks by leveraging image classification via CNNs. It is shown that the attack detection achieves high accuracy on the CIC-IDS2017 data set with reaction times of less than a second. Further, synthesized data sets have been used to evaluate detection capabilities of the approach, particularly, regarding less pronounced attack traffic characteristics (in terms of attack intensity). Furthermore, it is shown that filter rules for attack mitigation can be created by semantic image segmentation of the traffic images.

As the transfer of knowledge from the area of computer vision to the area of networking has shown promising first results, next steps include additional experiments regarding the effect of different image resolutions on the attack detection quality. Furthermore, adaptation of the aggregation scheme to similar attack patters (e.g., port scans) is considered. To achieve this, an extended set of aggregation features needs to be analyzed, including the port number space, inter-arrival times and packet lengths. Also time series of traffic aggregation maps will be considered, which can be compared to the classification of video sequences. The goal of observing and classifying time dependent images is to enable the ability of detecting changes in the traffic pattern over time, potentially leading to further improvements of reaction time.

Acknowledgement. This work was funded by the German Federal Ministry of Education and Research (BMBF), RefNr. 16KIS1142K. This work was supported by funding of the Helmholtz Association (HGF) through the Kastel Security Research Labs (POF structure 46.23.01: Methods for Engineering Secure Systems).

References

1. Intrusion detection evaluation dataset (cic-ids2017) (2017). https://www.unb.ca/cic/datasets/ids-2017.html
2. Deng, J., Dong, W., Socher, R., Li, L.J., Li, K., Fei-Fei, L.: ImageNet: a large-scale hierarchical image database. In: 2009 IEEE Conference on Computer Vision and Pattern Recognition, pp. 248–255 (2009). https://doi.org/10.1109/CVPR.2009.5206848

3. He, K., Zhang, X., Ren, S., Sun, J.: Deep residual learning for image recognition. In: 2016 IEEE Conference on Computer Vision and Pattern Recognition (CVPR), pp. 770–778 (2016). https://doi.org/10.1109/CVPR.2016.90
4. Jia, Y., Zhong, F., Alrawais, A., Gong, B., Cheng, X.: FlowGuard: an intelligent edge defense mechanism against IoT DDoS attacks. IEEE Internet Things J. **7**(10), 9552–9562 (2020). https://doi.org/10.1109/JIOT.2020.2993782
5. Kingma, D.P., Ba, J.: Adam: a method for stochastic optimization (2017)
6. LeCun, Y., et al.: Backpropagation applied to handwritten zip code recognition. Neural Comput. **1**(4), 541–551 (1989). https://doi.org/10.1162/neco.1989.1.4.541
7. Lecun, Y., Bottou, L., Bengio, Y., Haffner, P.: Gradient-based learning applied to document recognition. Proc. IEEE **86**(11), 2278–2324 (1998). https://doi.org/10.1109/5.726791
8. Leevy, J.L., Khoshgoftaar, T.M.: A survey and analysis of intrusion detection models based on CSE-CIC-IDS2018 Big Data. J. Big Data **7**(1), 1–19 (2020). https://doi.org/10.1186/s40537-020-00382-x
9. Liang, X., Znati, T.: A long short-term memory enabled framework for DDoS detection. In: 2019 IEEE Global Communications Conference (GLOBECOM), pp. 1–6 (2019). https://doi.org/10.1109/GLOBECOM38437.2019.9013450
10. Long, J., Shelhamer, E., Darrell, T.: Fully convolutional networks for semantic segmentation. In: Proceedings of the IEEE Conference on Computer Vision and Pattern Recognition (CVPR) (2015)
11. Malialis, K., Kudenko, D.: Multiagent router throttling: decentralized coordinated response against DDoS attacks. In: Proceedings of the Twenty-Seventh AAAI Conference on Artificial Intelligence AAAI 2013, pp. 1551–1556. AAAI Press (2013)
12. Ronneberger, O., Fischer, P., Brox, T.: U-Net: convolutional networks for biomedical image segmentation. In: Navab, N., Hornegger, J., Wells, W.M., Frangi, A.F. (eds.) MICCAI 2015. LNCS, vol. 9351, pp. 234–241. Springer, Cham (2015). https://doi.org/10.1007/978-3-319-24574-4_28
13. Simonyan, K., Zisserman, A.: Very deep convolutional networks for large-scale image recognition (2015)
14. Sudar, K.M., Deepalakshmi, P.: Flow-based detection and mitigation of low-rate DDoS attack in SDN environment using machine learning techniques. In: Nayak, P., Pal, S., Peng, S.L. (eds.) IoT and Analytics for Sensor Networks, pp. 193–205. Springer Singapore, Singapore (2022)
15. Wankhede, S., Kshirsagar, D.: Dos attack detection using machine learning and neural network. In: 2018 Fourth International Conference on Computing Communication Control and Automation (ICCUBEA), pp. 1–5 (2018). https://doi.org/10.1109/ICCUBEA.2018.8697702
16. Yu, F., Katz, R., Lakshman, T.: Gigabit rate packet pattern-matching using TCAM. In: 2004 Proceedings of the 12th IEEE International Conference on Network Protocols, ICNP 2004, pp. 174–183 (2004). https://doi.org/10.1109/ICNP.2004.1348108

ESOCC 2022 PhD Symposium

Preface to the ESOCC 2022 PhD Symposium

The PhD Symposium at ESOCC is an international forum for PhD students to present and discuss their work with senior scientists and other PhD students working on related topics. As for the main conference, the topics welcomed by the PhD Symposium span through all aspects of service-oriented and cloud computing, e.g., service and cloud computing models, service and cloud computing engineering, technologies, and business and social aspects of service and cloud computing. In contrast to the main conference, the research reports presented and discussed at the PhD symposium typically resume unfinished research work or present "just started" PhD research projects.

The Program Committee (PC) of the 2022 edition of the ESOCC PhD Symposium carefully selected two contributions out of the three submitted. The selection was based on the review reports on each submission, which were prepared by at least two PC members as part of a single-blind review process. The selected contributions carefully describe the research problem to be solved and preliminary results, as well as first ideas and future research directions towards solving the main problem. All these issues were discussed at the symposium with selected senior scientists and the PhD students. After the symposium, the PhD students were invited to incorporate all feedback from reviewers and from the live discussion at the PhD symposium in to their articles, to make such articles mature for a scientific publication. This post-symposium proceedings includes these revised selected articles.

We wish to thank the PhD students who contributed to the PhD symposium for their submissions and careful revisions of their articles, as well as the PC members and symposium attendees for their detailed and constructive feedback suggesting valuable improvements. We are also grateful to Wolf Zimmermann (General Chair of ESOCC 2022), Fabrizio Montesi and George Papadopoulos (Program Chairs of ESOCC 2022), and Guadalupe Ortiz and Christian Zirpins (Workshop Chairs of ESOCC 2022) for their organizational support, even in these troubled times. Without all the people mentioned above, such an enjoyable, virtual, and successful run of the 2022 edition of the ESOCC PhD Symposium would have not been possible.

May 2022

Jacopo Soldani
Massimo Villari

Organization

ESOCC 2022 PhD Symposium Chairs

Jacopo Soldani	University of Pisa, Italy
Massimo Villari	University of Messima, Italy

Program Committee

Uwe Breitenbücher	University of Stuttgart, Germany
Antonio Brogi	University of Pisa, Italy
Scharham Dustdar	TU Wien, Austria
Paul Grefen	Eindhoven University of Technology, Netherlands
Kung-Kiu Lau	University of Manchester, UK
Zoltan Adam Mann	University of Duisburg-Essen, Germany
Ulf Schreier	Furtwangen University, Germany

Improving the Key Exchange Process of the eXtended Triple Diffie-Hellman Protocol with Blockchain

Armando Ruggeri$^{(\boxtimes)}$ and Massimo Villari

MIFT Department, University of Messina, Messina, Italy
{armruggeri,mvillari}@unime.it

Abstract. The demand for safeguarding communications between people and equipment has been driven by recent breakthroughs in miniature smart data gathering devices. Traditional techniques based on key exchange protocols cannot be implemented by resource-constrained embedded devices, therefore the BlockChain-Based X3DH (BCB-X3DH) protocol, which is based on a resilient decentralization of the eXtended Triple Diffie-Hellman (X3DH) protocol, has been developed. This work extends the analysis to fit a generic Smart City scenario with Edge and IoT nodes, using intensive analysis on Raspberry Pi 3 model B+ and Raspberry Pi 4 to verify that the new protocol is not only resistant to well-known distributed attacks, but can also be executed by miniaturized hardware, saving resources, energy, and battery life.

Keywords: Blockchain · Cloud computing · Internet of Things · Edge computing · Smart contract

1 Introduction

With the rapid growth of Internet-connected devices, safeguarding communications between various parties (i.e., persons, devices, etc.) has become a must.

Any Information Technology (IT) system must guarantee that communications exchanged between parties remain confidential, that parties are trustworthy and legitimate, and that messages are sent solely to the intended recipient. Message encryption has been suggested and tested since Caesar's code, but Whitfield Diffie and Martin Hellman [1] proposed a key-exchange protocol based on arithmetic operations in 1976. It was very impossible to break with the processing capacity of the time using discrete logarithms, therefore this method has been used for over half a century.

Recently, an alternative to the Diffie-Hellman key exchange protocol, the eXtended Triple Diffie-Hellman (X3DH) [2], has been developed to overcome the impediment that parties must meet, physically or electronically, to exchange the seeds for the secret key. This protocol is built on a centralized trust architecture that uses a public key infrastructure (PKI) to store the participants' public keys, allowing for asynchronous agreement between offline parties.

© The Author(s), under exclusive license to Springer Nature Switzerland AG 2022
C. Zirpins et al. (Eds.): ESOCC 2022 Workshops, CCIS 1617, pp. 49–58, 2022.
https://doi.org/10.1007/978-3-031-23298-5_4

The objective of this research is to propose an alternative X3DH protocol based on Blockchain technology to eliminate the risk of Single Point of Failure (SPoF). Specifically, we propose the *BlockChain-Based X3DH (BCB-X3DH)* protocol [3] that permits to combine the well-known X3DH security mechanisms with the intrinsic features of data non-repudiation and immutability that are typical of Smart Contracts. In simple words, in BCB-X3DH, the centralized server used to perform agreements among parties is replaced by a distributed Blockchain network.

The designed Smart Contract generates a public/private key pair, saves the public key on the network, and transfers the encrypted private key to the requester without having to store it on the Blockchain. This is essential when a device with limited resources needs to encrypt and exchange data but is unable to produce the key pair.

The remainder of this work is structured as follows. Section 2 provides a summary of modern network communication security solutions. The motives for this study are highlighted in Sect. 3. The BCB-X3DH protocol's design, as contrasted to the regular X3DH protocol, is described in Sect. 4. Implementation details of different types of secure communications in IoT scenarios are discussed in Sect. 5. In Sect. 6, experimental analysis showing the differences in outcomes achieved between the BCB-X3DH and standard X3DH methods is contrasted. Finally, Sect. 7, highlights conclusions and the future works.

2   Background and Related Work

Due to the adoption of Smart Contracts to achieve trustiness, transparency, and traceability, Blockchain technology is being considered in both academic and industrial fields as a possible solution to resolve most security threats and privacy concerns in a heterogeneous application environment [4], and it should resolve many open information access issues [5,6]. Many scientific initiatives are underway in this context, to demonstrate how different Blockchain approaches can be used to replace single server architecture and how this configuration can be applied to communication security in a variety of domains, including the IoT context [7].

Because of the decentralized nature of Blockchain, it may be used to minimize the threat of DoS attacks while maintaining the secureness of the Smart Contracts [8].

The possible hazard of a new home and connecting a smart device to the home wifi is often underestimated [9], and these devices demand safer and more efficient communication protocols [10].

It is not simple to find the optimal balance of security, application, and energy efficiency, and each protocol necessitates some sacrifice.

In comparison to RSA encryption, several techniques based on Elliptic curve-based cryptography offer higher performance in terms of resource consumption to safeguard communications, and they are especially advised for resource-constrained IoT devices [11].

It has already been demonstrated that Blockchain and Smart Contracts may be used in a variety of scenarios to improve the system and network resiliency while retaining a high level of system trust due to the openness of the implementation details [12].

Compared to the previously mentioned research activities, this work proves, through practical implementation, how Blockchain technology can prevent the limitation of the SPoF and reduce the cyber threats, offering a trusted distributed service for IoT and low-resource devices.

3   Motivation

The weaknesses of the X3DH protocol can be summarized in two main fields: i) the intrinsic vulnerability against distributed attacks, and ii) the heavy computational consumption required to calculate the secret keys which can lead to a rapid discharging for battery-powered devices. As it is well known, a central server architecture is vulnerable to distributed attacks aimed at denying the offered services, by refusing to deliver a service or making the entire endpoint unreachable. Some of the most common attacks used by cyber-criminals are Man-in-the-middle (MITM) [13] and Distributed Denial of Service (DDoS) [14] attacks.

These are crucial in the X3DH application because a single server architecture is weak against such attacks. After all, attackers can get control over the server that manages the key exchange process, making the entire process unusable.

For what concerns the resource-efficiency for battery-powered devices, it must be considered that many small and resource-constrained IoT devices suffer from the possibility to spend enough resources on key generation.

The central server simply performs the key exchange after receiving the public keys from both participants. Hence, the key pair generation is performed by the IoT device. This can be a critical step and a limitation for low-cost embedded devices with limited memory, processing, and energy resources. For example, small embedded devices, running on a rechargeable battery and solar panels, might not have enough resources to spend for the key generation process as this will drain capacity from their main task, which is to collect data from sensors and share it.

However, it has been demonstrated that the X3DH protocol can be performed on-chain, lightening low-resource devices which can benefit from its indisputable security benefits [15].

The considerations discussed in this paper show that Blockchain might be a viable, trustworthy, and safe alternative to the traditional client-server architecture, including inherent security characteristics that would be difficult to develop and maintain in a traditional implementation.

Findings achieved for limited devices in a Smart City environment are analyzed in this work, and energy analysis is performed in terms of resources, battery capacity, and device lifespan to confirm the applicability of Blockchain-based X3DH solutions for low-resources devices.

4   Design

The server in charge of the key exchange procedure in the X3DH implementation must be trusted, and the counterparty's keys should only be transferred to the specified receiver. An attacker who gains control of the server renders the system inoperable, rendering the security procedure useless.

In the 1996 Diffie-Hellman key exchange protocol [1], Alice and Bob, two users, each define two arbitrary a and b values and two additional shared values: a prime number g and a primitive root modulus p. The complexity of logarithms mod g over a finite field $GF(g)$ with a prime number of elements g is what gives this process its security. A new approach based on Elliptic Curve cryptography has been proposed [2], with the feature of the key exchange process being performed asynchronously, allowing one of the users to remain offline.

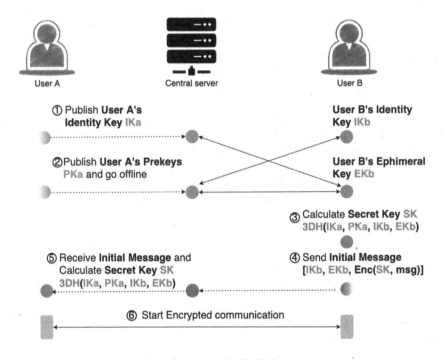

Fig. 1. eXtended Triple Diffie-Hellman scheme.

The new technique, depicted in Fig. 1, comprises a few phases that secure the Key Exchange mechanism's privacy. Users' signed prekey $SPKa$ and prekey signature $Sig(IKa, Encode(SPKa))$ is used by the first user to register with the central server using a Public Identity Key IKa and a set of Public keys known as Prekeys, specifically Users' signed prekey $SPKa$ and prekey signature $Sig(IKa, Encode(SPKa))$. User B can contact the central server to retrieve

User'A Prekeys, which are necessary to construct the Secret Key SK, as well as User's B Identity Key IKb and Ephemeral Key EKb.

User B sends his first message to the central server, called Initial Message, which contains his Identity Key IKb, the Ephemeral Key EKb used to produce SK, and a ciphered message encrypted with the SK. User A can download the Initial Message to extract the Public Keys needed to generate the same SK and start the secure communication between participants.

The battery-efficient BCB-$X3DH$ strategy has been investigated starting from the X3DH diagram in Fig. 1 to tackle the problem of the central server architecture and the limitation for low-resource and battery-powered devices.

Starting from the X3DH scheme, it is proposed an efficient application of the improved version of the $BlockChain$-$Based$ $X3DH$ $(BCB$-$X3DH)$ dedicated for low-resource devices that have not enough computational power to generate secret keys ensuring secure communication. Figure 2 schematizes its flowchart.

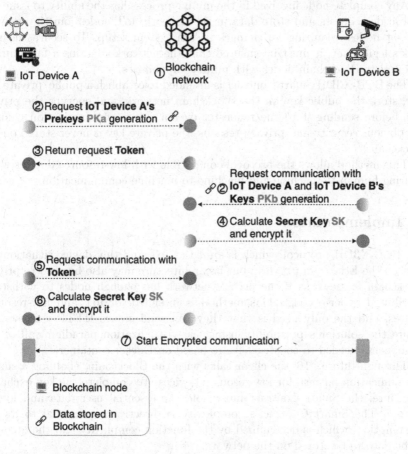

Fig. 2. BlockChain-Based eXtended Triple Diffie-Hellman flow diagram.

Through the use of a Smart Contract, the Blockchain network substitutes the central server to ease the key exchange process. Any user or generic IoT device may request a SK creation by sending a request to the Blockchain network, which will produce the Public Keys bundle for the requester and store it on the Blockchain for public access. IoT Device B must offer a pre-shared identify of the requested partner when it wishes to exchange a SK to secure communication with IoT Device A. If the Public bundle is accessible for IoT Device A, the Smart Contract generates the SK by combining the available Keys of both parties. If the bundle is unavailable because IoT Device A has not yet registered with the Blockchain network, the Smart Contract generates a unique ticket for the request that may be used to supply the SK when IoT Device A's Public keys become available. Secure encrypted communication can begin once both devices have received the SK.

The Blockchain network acts as a trustworthy server that stores data in an immutable manner. Blockchain nodes are the participants in the trading process.

Any complete node involved in the mining process has the ability to issue key generation requests and store data in the network. IoT nodes join the network as light nodes, requiring no changes to the system setup. To secure the network's legitimacy, it must be ensured that the network contains a fair number of complete Blockchain nodes with mining capabilities.

The BCB-X3DH Smart Contract is intended to establish a public/private key pair, store the public key on the Blockchain network, and encrypt the private part before sending it to the requester over a secure communication channel (for obvious security and privacy reasons, the private key is never stored on the Blockchain).

This method allows the protocol compatible with low-resource devices while securing human-to-machine and machine-to-machine communication.

5   Implementation

The BCB-X3DH protocol, which is aimed at IoT and tiny device situations, is built on the Ethereum network, but its architecture may also be used to private Blockchain frameworks if the private network has enough nodes to withstand distributed cyber-attacks. This method is intended for IoT and low-resource devices, and the only need is that they can send secure HTTP requests. To ensure the solution's portability using the virtualization paradigm, all of the components needed to construct it are based on Docker containers.

Through Infura, [16] the client talks with the Blockchain, enabling a simple communication pattern for low-resource devices. To complete the key exchange procedure, the Smart Contract must hold the essential user data and identification. The Smart Contract's complexity is directly proportional to its gas consumption, which is determined by the function complexity and the quantity of the data to be stored on the network.

Users or devices A and B simply need to know counter-party ID to start the key exchange procedure. If a device has adequate resources, it can build its key pair on its own or delegate the task to the Smart Contract. The Smart Contract is invoked to hold both parties' public keys and to carry out the agreement phase. It is worth noting that each user or device only pays a price in Ethereum cryptocoin (ETH) to keep their public key in the Blockchain network and that any data retrieval, such as getting the counter-party public key, is free. Hence, a device can exchange a secure key with an endless number of devices for the price of the initial public key submission. Once the Smart Contract is finished and the Secret Key is collected by both users and devices, it may be used to encrypt any communication through insecure channels.

6 Experiments

The experiments in this section are aimed at proving the resource efficiency of a Smart City scenario based on Blockchain technology in which several low-resource devices must interact across a secure channel. The experiments compare the power utilized locally and on-chain during the creation of key pairs using the Blockchain-based X3DH method provided in this paper.

The identity key IKa, the signed prekey $SPKa$, the one-time prekey $OPKa$, and finally, the Secret Key SK are generated using IoT Device resources in the classic X3DH approach based on a single third-party server; in the Blockchain-based X3DH solution proposed, the key pairs are generated on the Blockchain network through the Smart Contract, and the IoT Device's computation effort is negligible, as it only requires to perform an HTTP request.

The energy assessment was carried out with a Raspberry Pi 4 as the control unit, which was connected to the Texas Instruments INA219 sensor [17] through the I2C protocol.

This protocol is an asynchronous bus that uses two serial communication lines: the Serial DAta (SDA) for data communication and the Serial CLock (SCL) for clock communication. A reference line GND and a power connection line V must be utilized in addition to these two connections. The INA219 sensor detects the current flow in amps by measuring the voltage difference before and after the shunt, as well as the value of the resistor shunt (0.1 Ω).

In all approaches, performance is measured by the amount of time it takes to complete the key exchange operation. Two local IoT devices and a remote server running a complete Blockchain node are used in all testing. A Raspberry Pi 4 running Raspbian OS with a Quad-core Cortex-A72 64-bit SoC operating at 1.5 GHz and 4 GB RAM and a Raspberry Pi 3 Model B+ with a Quad-core 1.2 GHz and 1 GB RAM were utilized as IoT devices. The Ethereum Blockchain node is run on a Quad-core Intel® Xeon® 2.7 GHz remote server running Ubuntu Server 18.04 with 8 GB RAM. 100 read and write operations are assessed at 95% confidence intervals to evaluate both methodologies, and the average values are reported. Ropsten has been chosen as the official Ethereum public network for testing purposes to replicate a genuine server load status with more than 300 active nodes.

The average bus current required to complete the Key Exchange operation in the two implementations is shown in Fig. 3. The x-axis depicts the execution

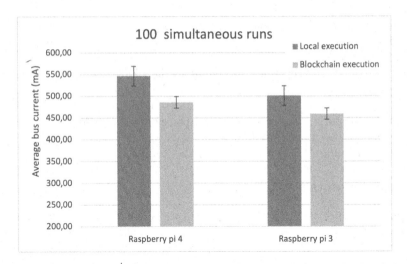

Fig. 3. Average bus current expressed in mA comparing the current intensity for key generation task performed locally and via the Smart Contract for different models of Raspberry Pi for 100 simultaneous runs.

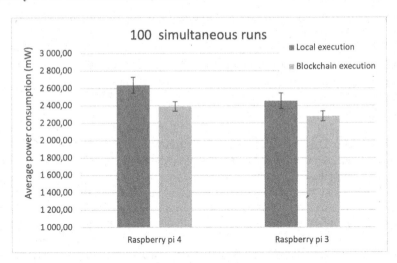

Fig. 4. Average power consumption expressed in mW comparing the power consumed for key generation task performed locally and via the Smart Contract for different models of Raspberry Pi for 100 simultaneous runs.

of 100 full Key Exchange procedures on a Raspberry Pi 4 and a Raspberry Pi 3 both locally and remotely via the Smart Contract. The current intensity is measured in milliamps on the y-axis (mA). The current intensity is always lower for the Raspberry Pi 3 execution since the resource utilized is always lower at idle state and much less for the remote execution based on the Ethereum Blockchain network for both IoT Devices, as shown in the graph.

Figure 4 shows a similar trend, showing the differing average power consumption required to complete the Key Exchange operation in the two implementations. The x-axis depicts the completion of 100 full Key Exchange procedures on the two IoT devices in question. The power usage is shown on the y-axis in milliwatts (mW). The graph illustrates a similar pattern, with the Raspberry Pi 3 consuming far fewer resources than other IoT devices, particularly when it comes to remote execution through Smart Contract.

According to the aforementioned findings, the remote Ethereum Blockchain-based solution uses less power, resulting in instant power energy savings, allowing resource-constrained battery-powered IoT Devices to extend their operating duration.

7   Conclusions and Future Work

This research investigates the energy consumption of IoT devices when a full eXtended Triple Diffie-Hellman Key Exchange protocol is used to exchange a Secret Key and secure communication over untrusted channels. Local execution and a remote Ethereum Blockchain node running on a dedicated Ubuntu Server are the two techniques investigated. This method allows the IoT Device to receive a safe Secret Key while just using the energy necessary to make an HTTP request, leaving all crypto-computation to the remote server. As a result, the IoT Device saves immediate resources and can survive longer in the event of battery-powered rechargeable through solar panels scenarios. Future analysis will be performed to validate the applicability of this approach for other IoT devices, such as NVIDIA Jetson Nano and Espressif ESP32, and to analyze new efficient consensus algorithms suitable for low-resource devices.

References

1. Diffie, W., Hellman, M.: New directions in cryptography. IEEE Trans. Inf. Theory **22**(6), 644–654 (1976)
2. Marlinspike, M., Perrin, T.: The x3dh key agreement protocol. Open Whisper Systems (2016)
3. Ruggeri, A., Celesti, A., Fazio, M., Galletta, A., Villari, M.: Bcb-x3dh: a blockchain based improved version of the extended triple diffie-hellman protocol. In: 2020 Second IEEE International Conference on Trust, Privacy and Security in Intelligent Systems and Applications (TPS-ISA), pp. 73–78. IEEE (2020)
4. Ruggeri, A., Fazio, M., Celesti, A., Villari, M.: Blockchain-based healthcare workflows in federated hospital clouds. In: Brogi, A., Zimmermann, W., Kritikos, K. (eds.) ESOCC 2020. LNCS, vol. 12054, pp. 113–121. Springer, Cham (2020). https://doi.org/10.1007/978-3-030-44769-4_9
5. Sengupta, J., Ruj, S., Bit, S.D.: A comprehensive survey on attacks, security issues and blockchain solutions for iot and iiot. J. Netw. Comput. Appl. **149**, 102481 (2020)

6. Sodhro, A.H., Pirbhulal, S., Muzammal, M., Zongwei, L.: Towards blockchain-enabled security technique for industrial internet of things based decentralized applications. J. Grid Comput. **18**, 1–14 (2020)
7. Zhang, P., White, J., Schmidt, D., Lenz, G., Rosenbloom, S.: Fhirchain: applying blockchain to securely and scalably share clinical data. Comput. Struct. Biotechnol. J. **16**, 07 (2018)
8. Puthal, D., Malik, N., Mohanty, S.P., Kougianos, E., Yang, C.: The blockchain as a decentralized security framework [future directions]. IEEE Cons. Electron. Maga. **7**(2), 18–21 (2018)
9. Santos, A.C., Soares Filho, J.L., Silva, Á.Í., Nigam, V., Fonseca, I.E.: Ble injection-free attack: a novel attack on bluetooth low energy devices. J. Ambient Intell. Humanized Comput., 1–11 (2019)
10. Sen, S.: Context-aware energy-efficient communication for iot sensor nodes. In: 2016 53nd ACM/EDAC/IEEE Design Automation Conference (DAC), pp. 1–6. IEEE (2016)
11. Suárez-Albela, M., Fernández-Caramés, T.M., Fraga-Lamas, P., Castedo, L.: A practical performance comparison of ecc and rsa for resource-constrained iot devices. In: 2018 Global Internet of Things Summit (GIoTS), pp. 1–6 (2018)
12. Singh, S., Sharma, P.K., Yoon, B., Shojafar, M., Cho, G.H., Ra, I.-H.: Convergence of blockchain and artificial intelligence in iot network for the sustainable smart city. Sustain. Cities Soc. **63**, 102364 (2020)
13. Mallik, A., Ahsan, A., Shahadat, M., Tsou, J.: Man-in-the-middle-attack: understanding in simple words. Int. J. Data Netw. Sci. **3**(2), 77–92 (2019)
14. Bhushan, K., Gupta, B.B.: Distributed denial of service (ddos) attack mitigation in software defined network (sdn)-based cloud computing environment. J. Ambient Intell. Humanized Comput. **10**(5), 1985–1997 (2019)
15. Ruggeri, A., Celesti, A., Galletta, A., Fazio, M., Villari, M.: An innovative blockchain based application of the extended triple diffie-hellman protocol for iot. In: 2021 8th International Conference on Future Internet of Things and Cloud (FiCloud). IEEE (2021)
16. Infura. https://infura.io/. Accessed 22 July 2021
17. INA219. Bidirectional Current/Power Monitor With I2C Interface. https://www.rototron.info/wp-content/uploads/INA219_datasheet.pdf. Accessed 22 July 2021

Towards Data Governance for Federated Machine Learning

José A. Peregrina[1,2]($\boxtimes$), Guadalupe Ortiz[1], and Christian Zirpins[2]

[1] Computer Science and Engineering Department, University of Cádiz,
Av. Universidad de Cádiz, 10, 11519 Puerto Real, Cádiz, Spain
guadalupe.ortiz@uca.es
[2] Faculty of Computer Science and Business Information Systems,
Karlsruhe University of Applied Sciences, Moltkestr. 30, 76133 Karlsruhe, Germany
{jose_antonio.peregrina_perez,christian.zirpins}@h-ka.de

Abstract. The application of Data Governance (DG) to Federated Machine Learning (FML) could enable support for improving the quality of Machine Learning (ML) models produced in a federation of participants belonging to different organizations. For that, we propose the adaptation of DG to provide such a support. The paper comprehends respective hypotheses, as well as the goals to prove their veracity. Then, a methodology to achieve the aforementioned goals is introduced. The paper also proposes a first approach of the conception that is currently taken as reference for the implementation process. The proposal aims to enable easier collaboration among participants belonging to different organizations, by providing mechanisms for improving quality of the machine learning models and enabling accountability in the federation. Finally, conclusions are drawn and the next steps of this research are outlined.

Keywords: Federated Machine Learning · Data Governance ·
Participants negotiation · ML model quality · Accountability

1 Introduction

Federated Machine Learning (FML) has created a new research field, as it allows participants to train jointly Machine Learning (ML) models without having to reveal the exact data being used for the training process or displace it outside the systems of the organizations involved. This is done by training a ML model with the participants' local data. During the training process, the different gradients computed by the participants are aggregated into a single gradient used for the back-propagation algorithm. The process is repeated until the global model achieves a good accuracy [4]. This approach is especially useful, as such organizations are not allowed to share personal data [13]. However, FML is not exempt of problems. A FML training process has new requirements like the need of the participants to agree on the problem being solved, the algorithm to use and the type of training data. All of this must be discussed without revealing sensitive

C. Zirpins et al. (Eds.): ESOCC 2022 Workshops, CCIS 1617, pp. 59–71, 2022.
https://doi.org/10.1007/978-3-031-23298-5_5

information, which would make the process unsuitable. Moreover, as there is a risk involved in the process, no organization will participate willingly unless some guarantees of quality and security are met. For this reason, mechanisms that allow to meet respective requirements are required.

Data Governance (DG) comprises different activities that focus on the distribution of responsibilities among the participants as well as support for the management of data. Nevertheless, this first definition goes for traditional DG and its adaptation to AI is not trivial. Some works [1,5] propose the steps to adapt DG to AI. A summary could be: Establishing what are the goals and quality requirements of the ML model, what are the responsibilities of the participants to this end and how the information related to the federation shall be properly managed by all participants. Despite the presence of related work on how to adapt DG to AI, there are still open problems remaining. First, there seems to be no adaptation of DG to FML, which possesses some different requirements. Second, there seems not to be an implementation that allows for all of this mechanisms in FML either. It is true that some proposals apply specific governance mechanisms, like accountability, in FML. Nevertheless, they lack functionalities to allow for the negotiation of training configurations and continuous improvement. Therefore, an application of this scope is still nonexistent.

The research described in this paper intends to conceive, design, implement and assess a DG system to support FML. Such architecture must support the aspects like the goals definition, the comparison among runs to reach better quality and access control to protect the information of the partners. By controlling these aspects, the participants can aim at defining and training high quality models that build on past experience in order not to repeat mistakes of the past and to research into how such a model could be improved. The main result will be the conception of the adaptation and application of DG for FML. Such conception will then be materialized in the form of an architecture to perform an assessment on the feasibility of the conception.

The rest of the paper is structured as follows: Sect. 2 explores the current state of the art. Section 3 describes the hypotheses of this research as well as the goals being pursued. Section 4 describes the methodology that will be followed throughout the research. Section 5 presents the first approach to the conception of DG applied to FML that is used as a reference for the implementation. Finally, Sect. 6 closes with some conclusions and a description of the following steps planned.

2   Related Work

Data Governance (DG) appears as a good solution for mechanisms regarding ML quality assessment or accountability. DG is defined as the different activities in charge of ensuring the correct management of data, the definition of responsibilities of the agents involved in such processes and the monitoring of all the actions performed to ensure the compliance with such activities. Kathri et al. [7] proposed five domains as a reference to design DG. When it comes to DG applied to AI, Janssen et al. [5] proposed multiple steps to control the quality of the AI models being governed within the system. The proposal only contemplates theoretically how to apply DG for ML within a company. Chandrasekaran et al. [1] proposes as well applying DG to ML, covering more aspects, and considering a perspective of different participants in the training. Yet, FML is not contemplated and it is only a theoretical approach. Different aspects like accountability, goal pursuing and model assessment are presented in his work, but as references to other previous works. There is no proposal for a system which could support all the needed functionalities to perform governance.

In a more technical view, Blockchain seems to be a common technology being used for governing the different FML processes. The term Blockchain refers to a distributed database with a tampering proof design, as every operation possesses a unique hash and some extra information, including the hash of the former element. Moreover, every single member of the network possesses a copy of all the operations. This makes trying to tamper the documents infeasible, as it would require to change all the documents of all the partners, including numerous expensive manipulations of interrelated hashes along the chain. Majeed et al. [8] proposed the use of Hyperledger Fabric channels and new protocols to govern a decentralized training process. Short et al. [11] uses the Blockchain for storing the hashes that point to the saved data in the server, for possessing a trace of all the operations being performed and he proposes a new protocol for checking that the quality of the model reaches a certain threshold of quality, although it only applies to accuracy. Mugunthan [9] specifies that the Blockchain is used to control some aspect about FML and to reward participants for their data in the form of tokens. Desai et al. [2] uses such tokens to punish participants that introduce poisoning attacks in the data. Finally, one piece of work offering different functionalities like FML and provenance over the training is *Substra* [3]. Nevertheless, none of these proposals unifies the data and model definition, quality measurements, policy definitions from the partners and possesses a metadata management system supporting the former functionalities.

3 Hypothesis and Goals

The overarching aim of this research is *to conceive, how Data Governance could be applied to support Federated Machine Learning*. An architecture will be designed, implemented and assessed to evaluate the conception. Such an architecture should allow partners to negotiate the data that will be used, to improve the quality of ML models and to define the different rules in the federation.

Despite the increasing popularity of FML, there are not many advances in how enterprises should collaborate to generate models and how better models can be pursued systematically in a federated way. Blockchain is usually the platform mentioned in terms of governing FML. This is mostly due to the fact that Blockchain incorporates smart contracts, allowing the partners to define the rules under the training process, write them in a smart contract and achieve traceability of the different operations within the network. Nevertheless, many Blockchain papers do not refer strictly to DG, nor try to apply all the formerly mentioned points, in order to ensure proper governance within the federation. The absence of methods to properly manage models and data between participants of different organizations, usually divided by administrative and/or organizational borderlines, and therefore under protection regulations, is what motivates this research. The underlying hypotheses are as follows:

- If Data Governance (DG) is applied to Federated Machine Learning (FML), it will improve the ML model development process.
- If DG is applied to organize a FML project, such organization will become more efficient.
- If DG is applied within the FML training and evaluation process, it will produce models of better quality.
- If DG is applied to FML, it will provide a safer environment to develop ML models in a federated fashion.
- From the conception of DG applied to FML, it is possible to create a framework that will enable the feasible application of DG.

In order to check the veracity of the hypotheses, this work will include both, a theoretical conception and a framework for *Federated Machine Learning Data Governance FML-DG*. The latter will be tested, in order to check its validity and whether it supposes an improvement over the existing solutions in both the market and the research community. Accordingly, the goals to achieve are enumerated below:

1. The first goal is to achieve a conception of how DG could be adapted to FML and therefore to prove the veracity or falsity of the aforementioned hypotheses. This conception should support all the shortcomings in the literature mentioned at the end of Sect. 2. Additionally, it should be usable as a reference on how to design an architecture to adapt DG to FML.
2. The second goal is to develop a software platform that can apply DG to FML before, during and after the FML process, in order to have control over the different operations in the federation. Such architecture will be based on the conception described in the first goal. The intended use is to assess the correctness of the conception.
3. The third goal is to perform an evaluation of the conception and the architecture in different real world scenarios. These are built around the federated training process therefore being ideal for the aforementioned assessment.

The first goal entails the theoretical conception of all the different elements that would compose the adaptation of DG to FML. Currently, in the literature, there is no precedent of any adaptation like this. Therefore, the limits of the adaptation within DG are also defined. Accordingly, the first goal is divided into the following sub-goals:

1.1 The concept of DG and how it can be applied to AI will be studied. This concept should enable us to understand how DG works and what are the necessary changes to also support the governing of ML.

1.2 The concept of FML and which are the requirements that any architecture of FML must achieve will be studied. This is necessary to understand the specific requirements that arise from the FML scenario, as it differs from usual ML.

1.3 The requirements of information sharing within a federation, in regards to the information needed for FML to work, will be studied. This information covers all the definitions that the partners may need to make regarding models, data and goals definitions, or additional regulations that they may want to enforce.

1.4 How the quality of models can be measured and improved for the intended use case will be studied. The different techniques for the improvement of models must be studied from the perspective of the federation, in which direct access to data is forbidden.

1.5 Which policies are necessary for FML will be investigated, in order to ensure the correct management of models and data, with compliance to the regulations, which may apply in this scenario.

1.6 What metadata is necessary for properly tracing the different operations in the federation will be investigated, as it acts as a support for the rest of aspects of DG.

1.7 The seventh and last sub-goal is to create the concept of how DG can be finally applied to FML. This goal will be achieved with the correct integration of all the aforementioned sub-goals in this first goal.

Departing from the different sub-goals of the conception, the following step is the design of a solution for the adaption. The development of an architecture is necessary in order to perform the required assessment over the conception of the application of DG to FML. Moreover, the appropriate evaluation process will be developed in order to ensure the correctness of the solution. For this, the second goal is divided into the following sub-goals:

2.1 The first sub-goal is to develop the components that are required to allow the partners to define and negotiate the different models to be trained and the data to be used. The different components here will be developed with the aim to allow different participants, in different scenarios, to create a successful FML process, ending with a satisfactory ML model.

2.2 The needed components to enforce policies over the federation will be developed, in order to forbid unauthorized operations. The different components here are in charge of forbidding any operation that goes against external or internal regulations, the latter being the ones defined and agreed by the participants of the process.

2.3 The third sub-goal is to develop the needed components to manage the generation and querying of metadata in the federation [10]. Metadata is a necessary and supportive element in DG. Therefore, it plays a fundamental role in every other aspect of the system.

2.4 The needed components to control the quality of the model and the data in the federation will be developed. The development of the components for quality must focus on the quality of the model and the data, both for immediate assessment and for further analysis from the participants. These components are the ones in charge of giving the participants the needed information to improve the resultant models.

2.5 The fifth and last sub-goal is to develop the rest of the components needed to merge all the previous designs into one overarching and integrated architecture. For this, the architecture must not only integrate all the aforementioned components, but also be of easy integration in any FML architecture.

Once the development has been completed, the assessment of both the conception and its materialization in terms of the architecture, can be performed. The third goal is divided in the following sub-goals:

3.1 Different characteristics of the system will be assessed, by experimentation with simulated data, in a simulated federation. Performance will be assessed, by calculating the overhead that the system produces when being integrated with a FML architecture. Scalability will be measured regarding how well the governance mechanisms perform when the number of participants vary. Additionally, other metrics may be included in the future in the assessment.

3.2 The second sub-goal is to evaluate the system in real world scenarios, in which the data is provided by different partners of the research group. The use cases include the following:

1. Fraud credit card detection.
2. Misuse of accounts.

These use cases will allow us to see how both the concept and the architecture behave in a real scenario and check whether it could work in a different scenario than these two.

3.3 The third and last sub-goal is to improve the system to work correctly, in case that in any of the former two sub-goals, the system presents a deficiency.

4 Methodology

The proposed research is divided into 4 stages. These stages satisfy the goals in Sect. 3. We describe the stages in the following subsections. Subsection 4.1 explains the activities regarding the study of the state of the art in both publications and tools available. Subsection 4.2 displays the activities related to the conception of the application of DG to FML. Subsection 4.3 describes the planned implementation steps of the DG solution. Finally, Subsect. 4.4 explains the steps that will be followed to assess the correctness of the implementation.

4.1 Study of the State of the Art

This first stage covers all the activities related to the study of the current state of the art regarding the application of Data Governance (DG) to ML, and especially the different aspects to both ML and Federated Machine Learning (FML).

During the first part of this stage an exhaustive literature study will be performed. This study will be related to both the concepts of FML and DG, the latter especially looking into applications of DG to AI. Then, the study will continue over the open problems that appear in FML that could be solved by adapting certain parts of DG. In case some of these problems are already solved, it is necessary to study how these solutions are applied and to discern whether they can be improved by the solution proposed in this research. This first part focuses on the first goal that is the conception of DG applied to FML. This literature research will serve to both the generation and validation of such a conception. After this stage is completed, periodical status checks of the state of the art will be performed, in search of new publications related to this work.

During the second part, once the different problems being aimed to be solved by our solution are spotted, a study will be carried out to collect the different existent tools to support the development. A few tools are needed within the federation in order to apply DG. One is a metadata management system, as metadata is an integral part of DG that acts as support for the rest of the parts. Also, a policy engine is required in order to set the minimum common policies for DG and to allow the partners to set the more sophisticated policies depending on the scenario. Finally, a federated learning architecture is essential in order to test the solution. Multiple types of architecture and their characteristics are to be studied to assess how the needs may change from one to the other. Some examples may comprehend centralized architectures, in which a server carries the aggregation process, like [4]. Others may propose decentralized architectures without a central server, like Substra [3]. This second stage focuses on solving the second goal, by providing the first approach for the development of a DG architecture.

4.2   Conception of Federated Machine Learning Data Governance

The second stage covers all the activities related to conceiving the adaptation of DG to FML. This theoretical conception aims to propose a concrete adaptation, as DG is a broad concept. Therefore, a DG model adapted to FML is to be produced.

The first part of this stage integrates with the first part of the former stage. As the problems are spotted, the conception can start taking shape. First, based on the literature already existent, it is possible to find examples of work that solve some of the problems this work aims at. Therefore, some work can be done by setting the related work as foundation. Then, based on the problems identified and chosen, part of the proposal about the adaptation can be done. This first part will cover all the specific problems regarding how to ensure that the concept allows to properly control both models and data to adapt it to the different use cases that may appear. For this, metadata will be generated. This model is produced to control information about data and models and to have traces of different operations. Also, the design will contemplate a policy engine to define restrictions on the operations in the federation. Finally, a way of assessing the federated models shall be integrated to then apply different governance mechanisms based on the quality of such models. This first part focuses primarily on the first goal, especially on sub-goals from 1.1 to 1.6.

The second part aims to take care of external problems that may shape our solution. One recurrent problem in a federation are the regulations in terms of data protection, like the GDPR [13]. The model must be then adapted to check which kind of information is necessary and helpful, and adapt its exchange to comply with the different regulations that may apply to this scenario. This aspect can be integrated in the policy engine. This second part focuses on every sub-goal of goal 1, as it is difficult to confirm that an external requirement will not affect a goal related task. Still, special focus will be given to sub-goal 1.4.

The third and last part shall cover the integration of all these aspects in a single model that will be used as foundation for the next stages. Therefore, this stage relates to the results being found in the second part of the first stage. Furthermore, the integration will be performed in line with the concept of DG, defining then one adaptation of DG to FML. It should be possible to use this conception as a basis for developing a DG framework that considers both internal and external problems. This last stage focuses on the sub-goal 1.7.

4.3   Development of the Data Governance Solution

The third stage covers all the activities related to both the design and implementation of DG-FML. There will be different parts in this stage. Nevertheless, the development methodology is not linear, but iterative and incremental.

The first part serves to start designing the solution based on the DG model developed in the former stage. The design that will be supported by the tooling researched in the first stage, must provide solutions for all these problems. Moreover, every piece of the design must aim to be easily integrated within an existing FML architecture. For each solution, the design should aim to provide an improvement over the already existent ones. The last part of the design would be the integration of the solutions into one, conforming the aimed adaptation of DG to FML. This stage covers all the related activities from sub-goal 2.1 to 2.4.

After the design, the second part will start the implementation-side of the development. First, a metadata management system will be implemented, to be able to save and compare different versions of models, data and training rounds, as well as a trace of the different operations being performed. Then, the next step is to define the minimum amount of policies needed for every scenario of FML. These policies will be implemented in the tool chosen. Following these two implementations, a way for the partners to agree on the models and data to be used will be implemented based on the tooling researched for such a purpose. Finally, based on a given method for measuring the quality of the data of the partners and on another method to assess the quality of the model, novel mechanisms to improve the quality will be implemented in the solution. Besides, every developed component shall be tested for correctness, in terms of unit or integration tests. This stage will be performed to reach the same sub-goals as the aforementioned design part.

The last development stage will be the integration of the implemented solution with federated training architectures. Therefore, the solution should possess capabilities to be easily connected to other systems. This will allow the system testing process to begin. Therefore, this last part focuses on the sub-goal 2.5, the last of the second goal.

4.4 Evaluation and Optimization, with Experimentation in both Simulated and Real Use Cases

The fourth stage will cover the different assessments of both the conception and the implemented solution by means of simulation and real world use cases.

On the one hand, the solution will be assessed by using simulated data in a simulated federation. This assessment will focus on different aspects regarding non-functional characteristics like performance and scalability. The simulated federation will vary its number of participants, to assess how much overhead the different governance mechanisms add to the federated training process. This overhead may show in the size of data stored or in the increase of response time. Additional metrics will be studied as appropriate. This part of the methodology focuses on solving the sub-goal 3.1.

On the other hand, different use cases, where partners separated by administrative borderlines want to train federated models, will be studied. These build the foundation for assessing feasibility in real world scenarios. In particular, security mechanisms for web-based systems are being investigated in the KIWI research project. The partners will be asked to use the solution of our work in order to organize a FML training process and to check whether the solution could help them improve the quality of the models produced.

In order to check the quality of the produced models in this environment, the experiments will be conducted on representative simulated data from the use cases. Additionally, metrics like fairness types will be included in the assessment, to ensure that the application of DG allows to build trustworthy models. Comparisons with the former models that these partners were using will be performed, to assess the effectiveness of our proposal. Such assessment will be necessary to achieve the sub-goal 3.2.

Corrections and improvements regarding performance, scalability and usability are expected to be made in this stage as well. These corrections will add to the completion of sub-goal 3.3.

5   A Preliminary Approach for FML-DG

This section introduces the first approach of the process to apply DG-FML. This is part of the first goal, which is aiming to the conception of DG-FML. This proposed approach for the process is part of the preliminary results achieved by following the aforementioned research methodology. Moreover, it is also being used as a reference to develop the architecture platform. The proposed approach can be seen in Fig. 1.

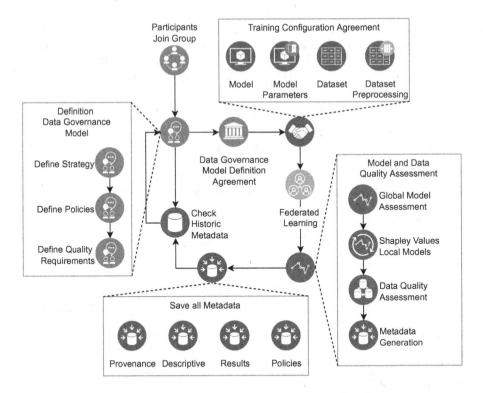

Fig. 1. Proposal for Data Governance applied to FML.

The process starts with the participants forming a *Group*. In each Group, there must be at least one responsible person per organization. Once the Group is formed, participants can start proposing *Data Governance Elements*. The main Data Governance Element is the *Strategy*, as the rest depend on it.

A *Strategy* expresses the goal being pursued by the group. This goal relates to the training of a ML model for a certain task. A *Strategy* is composed of three different aspects: *Policies*, *Quality Requirements* and *Training Configurations*. These aspects are described below.

The *Policies* respond to the restrictions that the participant may face due to the characteristics of the project. The need for Policies to control the operations of the FML process is still an open problem [14], despite some have already been proposed, like Verma et al. [15] proposing policies for the dataset name features, or PoliFL to impose a budget on differential privacy [6].

The *Quality Requirements*, agreed upon by the participants, must be achieved by the trained model. The Quality Requirements being researched so far are related to Correctness and Fairness [16]. Nevertheless, we consider to add more dimensions of the ML Quality Model [18] for the assessment of ML models.

Finally, and from the definition of the former three, different *Training Configurations* can be proposed by the participants. Each Training Configuration may possess different algorithms proposed (neural networks, decision trees, etc.) with different parameters. Also, the data being used for the training can be modified. In this case, as it is federated training, data cannot be shared among participants [13]. Therefore, an agreement regarding its structure and format must be reached without revealing any sensitive information.

Once all the participants have agreed on the Governance Elements, the FML process can start. The training should be carried out with the agreed Training Configuration. The evaluation process takes place during and after the training process. The importance of carrying it with the configuration is meant to enable an assessment on how changes on the Training Configuration (or other DG Elements) impact the resultant quality of the model [12].

The assessment step starts by evaluating the model based on the quality requirements defined by the participants. Depending on how the model performs for these quality requirements, a so called Shapley Values computation can be carried out [17]. This computation can enable the participant to check who is contributing the most and if someone may not be contributing at all. On the other hand, if mixed with additional data analysis activities, it can help understanding what kind of data is most valuable for the model being developed. In the end, quality is not an objective aspect, and the quality of the different elements depends on the problem being solved.

Across the full life-cycle, various types of *Metadata* are stored. During the Data Governance Elements definition and the Training Configuration agreement, *Provenance Metadata* regarding the Elements agreed is collected. The purpose of this is the comparison among the Configurations of training rounds. This provides required information to make changes that increase the quality of the resultant model [12]. Another important metadata type to be stored is related to the *ownership* of the proposals. Because the federation is formed by participants who may not trust others, allowing accountability during the process is essential to gain mutual trust [5,7]. Finally, *Descriptive Metadata* includes all information that allows the participants to better understand an Element in the federation.

Once the collection is completed, the participants can retrieve the metadata, and use it to plan the following training round, in case that the resultant model does not satisfy the quality requirements agreed.

In the future, this proposal will be polished with the aim of making it the conception of DG-FML. It will also be used as a reference for the development of the DG-FML architecture, allowing in the end for the testing of the conception. At the moment, there is already a vision of how blockchain concepts could help with the implementation of the proposal. The negotiation could take place off-chain in order to validate both, the model and the training configuration in-chain later on. Such model and configuration can be transformed into policies within a blockchain. Also, the training and the quality assessment can be orchestrated in a decentralized way by using the endorsement policies, by making the participants to exchange gradients among them or to upload the testing results into the blockchain. Finally, the configuration and the training results could be stored in the blockchain, making them public and accessible for all the participants.

Moreover, the functionality of channels can be used to hide the metadata from participants that do not belong to the specific group [8].

6   Conclusions and Future Work

This paper proposes a research plan for the adaptation of Data Governance to Federated Machine Learning, both on the conception and implementation level. The plan divides the two goals in subsequent sub-goals and later proposes the steps to follow for their successful completion. Finally, a first approach for Federated Machine Learning Data Governance (FML-DG) is proposed based on the research already performed.

Future work includes an application of the plan towards the final conception, implementation and assessment of FML-DG. Further research in the implementation of software components that allow the steps of the proposed approach to be performed, will be realized. Also, experimentation in real world use cases, in order to test the feasibility of the conception, will be conducted.

Acknowledgment. Funded by the German Federal Ministry of Education and Research. Project name: KIWI, RefNr: 16KIS1142K.

References

1. Chandrasekaran, V., Jia, H., Thudi, A., et al.: SoK: Machine Learning Governance (2021). http://arxiv.org/abs/2109.10870
2. Desai, H.B., Ozdayi, M.S., Kantarcioglu, M.: BlockFLA: accountable federated learning via hybrid blockchain architecture. In: Proceedings of the Eleventh ACM Conference on Data and Application Security and Privacy (CODASPY'21), pp. 101–112. Association for Computing Machinery, New York (2021). https://doi.org/10.1145/3422337.3447837
3. Galtier, M.N., Marini, C.: Substra: a framework for privacy-preserving, traceable and collaborative Machine Learning (2019). https://arxiv.org/abs/1910.11567
4. Hard, A., Rao, K., Mathews, R., et al.: Federated learning for mobile keyboard prediction (2018). http://arxiv.org/abs/1811.03604
5. Janssen, M., Brous, P., Estevez, E., et al.: Data governance: organizing data for trustworthy artificial intelligence. GIQ **37**(3), 101493 (2020)
6. Katevas, K., Bagdasaryan, E., Waterman, J., et al.: Policy-based federated learning (2020). http://arxiv.org/abs/2003.06612
7. Khatri, V., Brown, C.V.: Designing data governance. ACM **53**(1), 148–152 (2010)
8. Majeed, U., Hong, C.S.: FLchain: federated learning via MEC-enabled blockchain network. In: 2019 20th Asia-Pacific Network Operations and Management Symposium (APNOMS), pp. 1–4 (2019). https://doi.org/10.23919/APNOMS.2019.8892848
9. Mugunthan, V., Rahman, R., Kagal, L.: BlockFLow: decentralized, privacy-preserving, and accountable federated machine learning. In: Prieto, J., Partida, A., Leitão, P., Pinto, A. (eds.) BLOCKCHAIN 2021. LNNS, vol. 320, pp. 233–242. Springer, Cham (2022). https://doi.org/10.1007/978-3-030-86162-9_23

10. Peregrina, J.A., Ortiz, G., Zirpins, C.: Towards a metadata management system for provenance, reproducibility and accountability in federated machine learning. In: Zirpins, C., et al. (eds.) ESOCC 2022 Workshops, LNCS (CCIS), vol. 1617, pp. 5–18. Springer, Cham (2022). https://doi.org/10.1007/978-3-031-23298-5_1

11. Short, A.R., Leligou, H.C., Papoutsidakis, M., Theocharis, E.: Using blockchain technologies to improve security in federated learning systems, pp. 1183–1188. IEEE (2020)

12. Souza, R., et al.: Provenance data in the machine learning lifecycle in computational science and engineering. In: 2019 IEEE/ACM Workflows in Support of Large-Scale Science (WORKS), pp. 1–10 (2019). https://doi.org/10.1109/WORKS49585.2019.00006

13. Truong, N., Sun, K., Wang, S., et al.: Privacy preservation in federated learning: an insightful survey from the GDPR perspective. Comput. Secur. **110**, 102402 (2021)

14. Verma, D., et al.: Self-generating policies for machine learning in coalition environments. In: Calo, S., Bertino, E., Verma, D. (eds.) Policy-Based Autonomic Data Governance. LNCS, vol. 11550, pp. 42–65. Springer, Cham (2019). https://doi.org/10.1007/978-3-030-17277-0_3

15. Verma, D., White, G., de Mel, G.: Federated AI for the enterprise: a web services based implementation. In: 2019 IEEE ICWS, pp. 20–27 (2019)

16. Verma, S., Rubin, J.: Fairness definitions explained. In: Proceedings of the International Workshop on Software Fairness, pp. 1–7. ACM, NY (2018)

17. Wang, T., Rausch, J., Zhang, C., Jia, R., Song, D.: A principled approach to data valuation for federated learning. In: Yang, Q., Fan, L., Yu, H. (eds.) Federated Learning. LNCS (LNAI), vol. 12500, pp. 153–167. Springer, Cham (2020). https://doi.org/10.1007/978-3-030-63076-8_11

18. Zhang, J.M., Harman, M., Ma, L., Liu, Y.: Machine learning testing: survey, landscapes and horizons. IEEE Trans. Softw. Eng. **48**(1), 1–36 (2022). https://doi.org/10.1109/TSE.2019.2962027

ESOCC 2022 Projects Track

Preface to the ESOCC 2022 Projects Track

The ESOCC 2022 conference offered a useful opportunity for researchers to disseminate the latest research developments in their projects (EU Actions, NSF results, and more) and meet representatives of other consortia, sharing their progress and groundbreaking results. This year's Projects Track featured presentations focusing on a number of EU and national research project initiatives specifically supported by either Horizon Europe and/or national funding programs, with five interesting papers on topics ranging from cloud-based applied solutions to theoretical modelling for infrastructure code.

Each paper underwent a rigorous single-blind selection process involving three independent reviewers sampled according to their expertise. Additional reviewers were used for borderline papers to ensure that extensive feedback was provided to the authors and that a more rigorous selection and decisive process was instrumented. As a result of this process, each reviewer in the program committee was involved in the review of at most 1-2 submissions; this limited number ensured a form of appropriateness and quality for the provided review. The program featured two sessions structured as follows:

- Session 1 - Cloud Technologies
  - "QuickFaaS: Providing Portability and Interoperability between FaaS Platforms"
  - "Cloud Computing Continuum research topics and challenges. A multi-source analysis"
  - "Developing a New DevOps Modelling Language to Support the Creation of Infrastructure as Code"
- Session 2 - Applications and Meta-studies
  - "Urban Heat Island Detection Utilizing Citizen Science"
  - "Using a multi-sourced methodology to identify challenges in Software Technologies research"

June 2022   Damian A. Tamburri

Organization

ESOCC 2022 Projects Track Chair

Damian A. Tamburri   TU/e Eindhoven, The Netherlands

Program Committee

Dario Di Nucci   University of Salerno, Italy
Jacopo Soldani   University of Pisa, Italy
Pierluigi Plebani   Politecnico di Milano, Italy
Indika Kumara   Tilburg University, The Netherlands
Jose Merseguer   Universidad de Zaragoza, Spain
Marco Autili   University of Aquila, Italy
Christos Tsigkanos   University of Bern, Switzerland
Martin Garriga   YPF, Argentina
Giovanni Quattrocchi   Politecnico di Milano, Italy

QuickFaaS: Providing Portability and Interoperability Between FaaS Platforms

Pedro Rodrigues[1,2(✉)] ⓘD, Filipe Freitas[1,2] ⓘD, and José Simão[1,2,3,4] ⓘD

[1] IPL - Instituto Politécnino de Lisboa, Lisbon, Portugal
pedro-rodri@outlook.com
[2] ISEL - Instituto Superior de Engenharia de Lisboa, Lisbon, Portugal
[3] INESC-ID, Lisbon, Portugal
{filipe.freitas,jose.simao}@isel.pt
[4] Future Internet Technologies, ISEL, Lisbon, Portugal

Abstract. Serverless computing hides infrastructure management from developers and runs code on-demand automatically scaled and billed only during code's execution time. One of the most popular serverless back-end service is called Function-as-a-Service (FaaS), in which developers are many times confronted with cloud-specific requirements mainly due to the usage of specific function signatures and unique libraries. In this work, we introduce QuickFaaS, a multi-cloud interoperability desktop tool targeting cloud-agnostic functions development and FaaS deployments. QuickFaaS substantially improves developer's productivity, flexibility and agility when developing serverless solutions to multiple cloud providers, contributing to vendor lock-in mitigation as well as reducing portability related issues.

Keywords: Cloud interoperability · Cloud orchestration · Serverless computing · Cloud-agnostic functions · FaaS portability

1 Introduction

Serverless computing was a major technological breakthrough that has been drawing interest from the industry as well as academic institutions [1], largely due to the recent shift of enterprise application architectures to containers and microservices. Serverless potential is sustained by the great abstraction of server management challenges with low costs, which leads to the growth of the global Function-as-a-Service (FaaS) development. Cloud providers assume most of the responsibilities when it comes to serverless computing, in a way that the development of systems can be more focused on business logic and less on non-functional aspects, such as elasticity and load balancing.

Multi-cloud strategies provide organizations a better reliability to their services by preventing single points of failure in case of a cloud provider going down

Work supported by *Instituto Politécnico de Lisboa - IPL/2021/FaaS-IntOp_ISEL*.

C. Zirpins et al. (Eds.): ESOCC 2022 Workshops, CCIS 1617, pp. 77–82, 2022.
https://doi.org/10.1007/978-3-031-23298-5_6

[4]. Poly cloud is often mistaken for multi-cloud. In a poly cloud approach, the system benefits from services of different cloud providers that best suit a specific use case, targeting different cloud providers in exchange for a functional benefit. For the purposes of this work, we will consider both strategies in the same manner and use the term "multi-cloud" in application of either scenario.

Each cloud provider has its own requirements for the development of serverless functions. The noticeable tight-coupling between providers and serverless function services amplifies various vendor lock-in problems that discourage developers and organizations to migrate or replicate their serverless applications to different cloud providers. As mentioned by the Research Cloud group of the Standard Performance Evaluation Corporation (SPEC) [2]:"There is a need for a vendor-agnostic definition of both the basic cloud-function and of composite functions, to allow functions to be cloud-agnostic".

To the best of our knowledge, no published work suggests an approach to characterize and model cloud-agnostic FaaS applications while avoiding the installation of provider-specific tooling. Nonetheless, there are already a couple of cloud orchestration tools that provide a better management of multi-cloud environments. Terraform is probably the developer's number one choice for an infrastructure as code (IaC) tool. However, it is far from being cloud-agnostic when it comes to function development and deployment since each cloud provider has its own dedicated configuration file (*.tf) that needs to be strictly followed. Serverless Framework ends up sharing the same types of problems of Terraform by having deployment models that are not cloud-agnostic, they describe provider-specific services, event types, etc. Pulumi introduces a new approach for simplifying the development of cloud functions in the form of lambda expressions, they call it *Magic Functions*. However, both the signatures as well as the libraries that are required for *Magic Functions* are not cloud-agnostic.

2   Challenges in FaaS Adoption

We identified a few challenges when adopting FaaS solutions: each cloud provider (i) uses custom function signatures, (ii) provides unique libraries that introduce various dependencies, (iii) decides which deployment environment is required, (iv) has different deployment configurations to be established and (v) uses different service naming terminologies. To evidence the differences between function signatures, exemplified below, in Listings 1.1 and 1.2, are two simple cloud functions written in Java. Both functions are triggered via HTTP requests and can be deployed in MsAzure and Google Cloud Platform, respectively.

Listing 1.1. MsAzure cloud function

```
public class Function {
  @FunctionName("HttpExample")
  public HttpResponseMessage run(
    @HttpTrigger(
      name = "req",
      methods = {HttpMethod.GET},
      authLevel =
        AuthorizationLevel.ANONYMOUS)
      HttpRequestMessage request,
      ExecutionContext context) {
    return request
      .createResponseBuilder(200)
      .body("Hello world!").build();
  }
}
```

Listing 1.2. GCP cloud function

```
public class Function implements HttpFunction {
  @Override
  public void service(HttpRequest request,
    HttpResponse response) throws IOException
    {
    BufferedWriter writer = response.getWriter();
    writer.write("Hello world!");
  }
}
```

By introducing such wrapping around the actual business logic, functions can become deeply dependent on provider's requirements.

3   QuickFaaS

QuickFaaS is a multi-cloud interoperability desktop tool targeting cloud-agnostic functions development and FaaS deployments, contributing to vendor lock-in mitigation by improving function's portability. We adopted a top-down approach to design a couple of entity relationship models (ERMs). The more abstract ERM in Fig. 1 illustrates the three main blocks that compose QuickFaaS's solution.

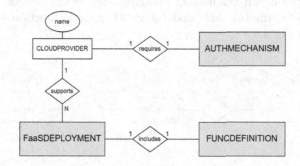

Fig. 1. Abstract ERM of the solution

Initially, QuickFaaS will support FaaS deployments to GCP and MsAzure. The expansion to other cloud providers is feasible. They both share similar implementations of services based on the industry-standard protocol for authorization OAuth 2.0: Google Identity and Ms Identity Platform. QuickFaaS benefits from this common mechanism to authenticate its users in those providers, avoiding the need to require the installation of extra tools for authentication purposes. In order to receive access tokens sent by providers, QuickFaaS launches an HTTP server that starts listening for requests locally on a certain port.

FaaS deployments can be challenging when dealing with multiple providers that require the setup of different types of configurations and environments. QuickFaaS tries to overcome these types of adversities by only enabling the setup of fundamental configurations that are present in most cloud providers. Some provider-specific configurations are possible to be modified, but only the ones that are considered relevant or can affect the function's performance, e.g., the memory allocated. Usually, a FaaS needs to be linked to a storage resource, we adopted the same naming terminology from AWS and GCP by calling it a bucket. The user must have at least one bucket created before being able to deploy a FaaS. Similarly to the authentication process, QuickFaaS benefits once again from a common mechanism available in the supported cloud providers, avoiding the need to require extra tooling for deployment. The mechanism works by uploading a ZIP archive using provider-specific APIs. The ZIP archive contains all the necessary artifacts to successfully launch the serverless function in the cloud.

3.1   Function Definition

The definition of a cloud function has a considerable impact when dealing with portability related issues in a serverless application. This is mainly due to FaaS platforms having to impose the usage of provider-specific function signatures as well as libraries. One of the key features offered by QuickFaaS is the development of cloud-agnostic functions, that is, functions that can be reused in multiple cloud providers without the need of changing a single line of code. The entities and respective attributes that model a cloud-agnostic function definition are represented in Fig. 2.

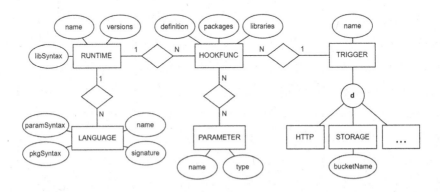

Fig. 2. ERM - function definition

Every cloud function needs a provider-specific signature in order to get triggered by a certain event, so how can cloud providers handle the execution of cloud-agnostic functions? To overcome this restriction, we adopted the behavioral design pattern, identified by Gamma, called the *Template Method Pattern* [3]: "The *Template Method* lets subclasses redefine certain steps of an algorithm without changing the algorithm's structure". In our case, the template method-/function is the entry point of the deployed FaaS, that is, the function that follows the provider-specific signature and gets triggered by a certain event. The cloud-agnostic function, developed by the QuickFaaS user, corresponds to the *hook* function specified in the *Template Method Pattern*. The term "*hook*" is applied to functions that are invoked by template functions at specific points of the algorithm. QuickFaaS provides a built-in code editor for the development of *hook* (cloud-agnostic) functions. Template functions are predefined in QuickFaaS and don't require any modification by the user. Template functions, unlike *hook* functions, are specific to a cloud provider due to requiring the usage of custom function signatures and provider-specific libraries.

Below, in Listings 1.3 and 1.4, we exemplify the usage of the *Template Method Pattern* for the provider GCP, by implementing both the template function and a *hook* function, respectively, using the Java programming language. The template function follows a provider-specific signature so that it can be triggered by an HTTP request.

Listing 1.3. GCP template function

```
public class Function implements HttpFunction {
    @Override
    public void service(HttpRequest request,
        HttpResponse response) {
    HttpRequestQf reqQf =
        new GcpHttpRequest(request);
    HttpResponseQf resQf =
        new GcpHttpResponse(response);
    // Calls the hook function
    new MyFunctionClass().myFunction(reqQf, resQf);
    }
}
```

Listing 1.4. Hook function

```
public class MyFuncClass {
    public void myFunc(
        HttpRequestQf req,
        HttpResponseQf res) {
    res.send(200, "Hello
        world!");
    }
}
```

The developer should embrace the libraries provided by QuickFaaS when writing a fully cloud-agnostic function. In the above example, these libraries correspond to *HttpRequestQf* and *HttpResponseQf*. Even though the libraries may look cloud-agnostic from the user's perspective, under the hood they are interacting with unique APIs from cloud providers to execute specific operations. The developer has the option to specify a list of external libraries by using a certain syntax that varies depending on the runtime.

4 Conclusion and Future Work

In this work, we presented QuickFaaS, a multi-cloud interoperability desktop tool targeting cloud-agnostic functions development and FaaS deployments. The main contributions of this project are: (i) the usage of a common authentication mechanism available in every provider, (ii) the possibility of developing reusable cloud-agnostic functions and (iii) the convenience of deploying a FaaS without the need of requiring the installation of extra provider-specific tools.

Since this is an on-going project, some of the models illustrated in this work can eventually be updated with a few more details. As a future work, we plan on continuing the development of QuickFaaS as well as exploring appropriate use cases that could highlight even more the benefits of the tool and its models.

References

1. Castro, P., Ishakian, V., Muthusamy, V., Slominski, A.: The rise of serverless computing. Commun. ACM **62**(12), 44 (2019). https://doi.org/10.1145/3368454
2. van Eyk, E., Iosup, A., Seif, S., Thömmes, M.: The SPEC cloud group's research vision on FaaS and serverless architectures. In: Proceedings of the 2nd International Workshop on Serverless Computing, pp. 1–4 (2017). https://doi.org/10.1145/3154847.3154848
3. Gamma, E., Helm, R., Johnson, R., Vlissides, J.: Design Patterns: Elements of Reusable Object-Oriented Software. Addison-Wesley, Boston (1995)
4. Petcu, D.: Multi-cloud: Expectations and current approaches. In: Proceedings of the 2013 International Workshop on Multi-Cloud Applications and Federated Clouds, pp. 1–6 (2013). https://doi.org/10.1145/2462326.2462328

Cloud Computing Continuum Research Topics and Challenges. A Multi-source Analysis

Juncal Alonso⬤, Leire Orue-Echevarria⬤, and Enrique Areizaga(✉)⬤

TECNALIA-BRTA, Astondo Bidea, Edificio 700, 48160 Derio, Bizkaia, Spain
Enrique.areizaga@tecnalia.com

Abstract. While the emergence of COVID-19 [1] has put major cloud service providers around the world to the test, the pandemic has also provided a strong impetus for the adoption and deployment of cloud computing: the transition to a remote workforce, entertainment, e-commerce, and especially remote education have affected the cloud industry and how providers are responding to the sudden and significant increase in demand for cloud solutions and services. Obviously, while highlighting the robustness of the public cloud, the pandemic-induced situation also highlights several important research challenges that need to be addressed.

This paper presents a multi-source based analysis for the identification of cloud computing research challenges as part of the road mapping methodology followed in the HUB4CLOUD project. The analysis consists of an in-depth study of several sources including analysis of the international context, analysis of academic venues, interviews with relevant stakeholders and existing funded projects.

The paper also provides an overview of the main research topics identified and proposes next steps for the utilization of these finding in the development of a Cloud Computing research roadmap.

Keywords: Cloud computing · Research topics · Multi-source analysis · Cloud continuum

1 Introduction

HUB4CLOUD [2] is a Coordination and Support Action (CSA) whose main ambition is to contribute to transform the current community of cloud computing researchers and innovators in Europe into an increasingly cohesive, dynamic, participatory and sustainable ecosystem, playing an important role in contributing to the technological ambitions of the next generation Internet. One of the main objectives of HUB4CLOUD is to coordinate the strategic and prospective planning of the entire European Cloud Computing (ECC) ecosystem to provide indications and recommendations for future (public and private) investments in next generation cloud computing. To this end, it will lead strategic research and innovation roadmapping and policy recommendation activities through close collaboration with the European Commission, as well as with other ongoing and future ECC projects and related initiatives. This document presents the main methodology for implementing these roadmaps, focusing especially on the first step of the methodology (Analysis and identification of research topics).

C. Zirpins et al. (Eds.): ESOCC 2022 Workshops, CCIS 1617, pp. 83–87, 2022.
https://doi.org/10.1007/978-3-031-23298-5_7

2 Methodology

The multi-source analysis presented in this paper covers the first pillar of the HUB4 CLOUD methodology shown in Fig. 1.

Fig. 1. Pillars of the roadmapping and policy recommendation methodology

In this first step, HUB4CLOUD has analyzed several initiatives to understand the context and landscape. These initiatives are not only in Europe and include Gaia-X, IPCEI-CIS or the European Alliance for Data, Cloud and Edge, but it also analyzes those in the United States and China. In the case of the United States, it has focused on the analysis of NSF-funded research projects, while in China, HUB4CLOUD has approached companies to find out their feeling towards cloud computing. In addition, the context analysis also includes consultation and surveys conducted in the framework of funded projects in the field of "cloud computing", experience and insights gathered from the H-Cloud CSA and interviews conducted with selected stakeholders from key organizations in the cloud and open-source domain. Once the context was understood, the research topics were extracted following a systematic and reproducible approach, in, which more than 30 journals and articles from among 100 research venues were thoroughly reviewed. The academic venues (journals and conferences) were selected based on the own experience of the Hub4Cloud partners and Google Scholar under "Engineering and Computer Science > Computing Systems [6]" (Fig. 2).

From these sites, and from the inputs from the context analysis, seven broad themes have been identified and described. Their description also includes the expected time frame in which they could be realized and their impact in technological, societal and business terms (Fig. 3).

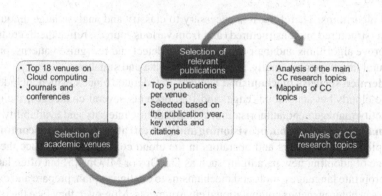

Fig. 2. Methodology followed for the analysis of academic publications.

3 Cloud Computing Continuum Research Topics and Challenges

The following is a brief description of the initial set of research themes and challenges. While the primary source of the research challenges is the analysis of research venues, it has been complemented by inputs from context analysis, surveys, interviews, and research projects. The full description of the research challenges can be found in [4].

1. **Compliance as code:** Compliance as code ensures that all regulatory compliance requirements are met by using tools to automatically configure requirements and then collect, gather evidence, and evaluate that evidence against a set of pre-defined metrics/requirements. Compliance-as-code enables the prevention, detection, and remediation of non-compliance, especially when high levels of security assurance are sought. In this sense, compliance as code for organisational measures (e.g. policies and procedures), which involve natural language processing and the need for machine-readable language and a large corpus of data, is a challenging task. Finally, the characteristics and complexity of the cloud supply chain make the task of compliance-as-code even more complex, as certifications will also need to be composed.

2. **Federation of Clouds** (including edge nodes, IoT and other infrastructural resources with sufficient computational power): Cloud federation presents several challenges not only from a technical point of view but also from an operational point of view that, in the end, also affect the technical solution adopted: Common description model of multi-layer resources, mechanisms and protocols for verification of service and instance credentials in their lifecycle, mechanisms for dynamic stateless and stateful portability of data and applications, etc.

3. **Optimization techniques for the Cloud Continuum**: The use of heuristics and evolutionary algorithms has great potential to improve non-functional characteristics of various domains of the cloud continuum, such as minimising energy consumption, minimising latency or optimising resource allocation.

4. **Cognitive Cloud Computing:** The goal with cognitive computing in the cloud is to mimic the decision making that a DevOps team member would do in a given situation and execute that decision automatically using artificial intelligence techniques

and algorithms. Therefore, it is necessary to classify and analyse large amounts of data (structured and unstructured) and from various sources, refine them, create and improve algorithms and their execution time, detect and recognise patterns, process natural language and, finally, self-learn from data and situations.

5. **Federated security mechanisms:** Security in federated clouds, which include multiple clouds but also cloud, edge, and fog, presents several challenges, including: Identity management, authorisation, confidentiality, integrity and availability.

6. **Dynamic configuration, provisioning and orchestration in the cloud continuum:** Application developers and operators in the cloud continuum today face the challenge of adopting new paradigms such as DevOps or MLOps [5] but often lack the appropriate languages, tools and mechanisms to configure, plan, prepare and execute tasks in heterogeneous computational environments. Moreover, they face the tasks of continuous optimisation and autonomic (re)deployment of complex, context-aware and stateless applications and data in a federated environment (including edge, cloud and network services) ensuring service continuity and anticipating possible failures in the underlying infrastructure, especially in critical systems that need to be resilient and whose response time becomes vital.

7. **Data Governance Frameworks:** Data is becoming the new asset of organisations. The creation of sectoral and cross-sectoral data spaces is expected to become a reality. However, there are still challenges to be solved: Implementation of data use policies, Enforcement of data use policies, Traceability, Monetisation and revenue models for data sharing, Data sharing mechanisms, Privacy preserving technologies, multiparty computing (MPC), homomorphic encryption, differential privacy, obfuscation, privacy risk assessment, technical and semantic interoperability.

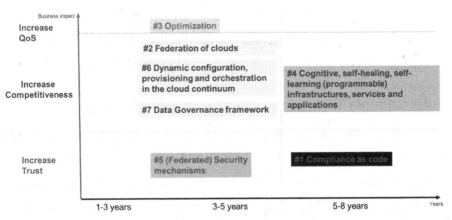

Fig. 3. Overview of identified cloud computing continuum research topics. Source: [4].

4   Conclusions

This paper has presented HUB4CLOUD's multi-source analysis for the identification of cloud computing research challenges.

The paper presents the methodology followed and the main sources analysed. It also discusses the research topics identified and provides a graphical representation of the expected timeframe in which they could be realised, as well as their impact in terms of business. As next steps, the main research topics identified will be ranked following a multi-factor ranking methodology and prioritised through public consultation. These research topics will be the main input for the implementation of the European Cloud Computing Roadmap in HUB4CLOUD.

References

1. Sayegh, E.: As COVID-19 Pushes Businesses to Their Limit. The Cloud Rises Above, FORBES, 26 March
2. HUB4CLOUD. https://www.h-cloud.eu/ict_40-projects/hub4cloud/. Accessed 03 March 2022
3. H-cloud. https://www.h-cloud.eu/. Accessed 03 March 2022
4. HUB4Cloud consortium. D1.4 Contributing to the European Cloud Computing Strategic Research and Innovation Agenda Q3–2021 (2021)
5. Ruf, P., Madan, M., Reich, C., Ould-Abdeslam, D.: Demystifying MLOps and presenting a recipe for the selection of open-source tools. Appl. Sci. **11**, 8861 (2021). https://doi.org/10.3390/app11198861
6. https://scholar.google.com/citations?view_op=top_venues&hl=en&vq=eng_'computingsystems

Developing a New DevOps Modelling Language to Support the Creation of Infrastructure as Code

Michele Chiari[1](✉) ⓘ, Elisabetta Di Nitto[1] ⓘ, Adrián Noguero Mucientes[2], and Bin Xiang[1] ⓘ

[1] DEIB, Politecnico di Milano, Milano, Italy
{michele.chiari,elisabetta.dinitto,bin.xiang}@polimi.it
[2] Go4IT Solutions, Parque Tecnológico Bizkaia, Bilbao, Spain

Abstract. The deployment of cloud applications and the correct management of their lifecycle is a colossal task. Infrastructure as Code (IaC) tools make this task easier; however, they require the user to have a deep knowledge of both the IaC language and the characteristics of various cloud services providers. The PIACERE project has developed a DevOps Modelling Language (DOML), aiming at describing cloud applications that are agnostic of the specificities of the different providers and IaC tools used for provisioning, deployment and configuration. DOML provides several modeling perspectives in a multi-layer approach. An application can be described in three layers: application layer, abstract and concrete infrastructure layer. It allows developers to describe how cloud applications are structured in an abstract manner, mapping the different software components to the concrete infrastructure elements, enabling the usage of different concretizations to match one particular deployment. This paper provides an overview of the DOML language: its layers and extension mechanisms, as well as an example to showcase its modeling capabilities.

Keywords: Infrastructure as code · DevOps modelling language · Multi-layer approach · Abstraction

1 Introduction

IaC (Infrastructure as Code) [1] has introduced the possibility to program beforehand the way software is deployed and configured on some execution environment composed of Virtual Machines (VMs) and/or various kinds of containers. Thanks to this IaC programming effort, it is possible to replicate a deployment multiple times by just running a script, to keep the characteristics of the operational environment under control, to better maintain the applications, and to speed up the time to market for a product.

However, building IaC is not a trivial task. It requires an in-depth knowledge of both the IaC language to be used and the characteristics of the target operational environment.

This project has received funding from the European Union's Horizon 2020 programme under grant agreement No 101000162 (PIACERE).

The PIACERE project [2] aims at allowing DevOps teams to model different infrastructure environments, by means of abstractions, through a DevOps Modelling Language (DOML) that hides technicalities of current solutions and increases productivity. Models defined in the DOML are then translated, through the Infrastructural Code Generator (ICG), into the target languages needed by the existing IaC tools, to reduce the time needed for creating infrastructural code for complex applications.

DOML models are created through the PIACERE IDE, which supports users in their activities with suggestions and guidance, integrating all design-time PIACERE tools.

Another issue is that, in the current highly dynamic and evolving context, new computing resources and new IaC languages and tools are continuously emerging. This requires extensibility mechanisms for the DOML and the corresponding ICGs to ensure the sustainability and longevity of the PIACERE approach and tool-suite. To this end, the DOML Extension mechanisms (DOML-E) will allow new infrastructural components and IaC tools to be incorporated in the DOML language for software execution, network communication, cloud services, or data storage.

2 Current IaC Approaches

The IaC area includes several different languages and runtime environments that focus on specific aspects of the whole problem of automating deployment and runtime management of complex applications. For instance, prominent languages today are Terraform [3] and TOSCA [4], mostly focusing on provisioning of resources in multiple cloud environments, Ansible [5], Chef [6] and Puppet [7] mostly tackling the problem of configuring VMs and on deploying software layers on top of them, the Dockerfile [8] language for controlling the creation of execution containers that can be used on top of any operating system to decouple a software component from low level details, the Kubernetes [9] configuration language to customize the operational environment features that support monitoring, autoscaling, restart of components.

In summary, there is a large variety of competing approaches requiring the adoption of different programming languages for writing infrastructural code. All these are focusing on a single or a small set of automation steps and of resource types (e.g., VMs). They mostly focus on cloud computing, leaving aside other computational resources such as those at the edge. Thus, there is not really an end-to-end solution covering all aspects and developers are forced to use a combination of different languages and tools.

3 DOML Modelling Principles

We are developing the DOML as a high-level modelling approach that is mapped into multiple IaC languages addressing specific aspects of infrastructure provisioning, and application deployment and configuration. We describe a preliminary DOML version in [10]. We now present the principles guiding our approach.

3.1 A Single Model for Multiple IaC Code Fragments

In the definition of the DOML, we aim at enabling users to create models that can result in IaC code written in different languages and dedicated to executing different operations. E.g., let us assume that we create a DOML model representing the UML diagram shown in Fig. 1. Here we adopt the UML graphic notation to formulate examples intuitively. The DOML syntax, however, is not based on UML, because UML contains an extremely wide variety of features, most of which are not useful for describing infrastructural deployments. Instead, the DOML aims to be a textual language specifically targeted at IaC. The diagram shows a component A that requires the installation of NodeJS for its execution. In turn, NodeJS is running on a Docker container on a VM.

Fig. 1. Relationships between a component and the execution environment it runs on.

We can infer that the following steps must be performed to deploy and run the system:

1. A container image must be created, incorporating NodeJS and component A.
2. A VM with the required characteristics must be provisioned and associated to a public IP address; this step can be executed in parallel with the previous one.
3. A Docker engine must be deployed in the VM.
4. The container image must be run on the VM by the Docker engine.

Then, the web server and component *A* can start their execution.
These steps can be accomplished if we generate the following artifacts:

- A Dockerfile that manages the creation of the container image (step 1)
- A Terraform or TOSCA blueprint in charge of orchestrating steps 2 to 4, interacting with the VM provider and executing all needed scripts.
- Some Ansible playbooks or similar scripts that execute steps 3 and 4.

Besides the complexity of the individual files to be created, an important issue we note is that these files are all written using different languages featuring a different programming model. With DOML we would like to understand the extent to which the scripts needed to accomplish the above steps can be derived from a high-level model with the components identified in Fig. 1, thus limiting the need for the end users to work with the target languages as much as possible.

3.2 Separation of Concerns and Multiple Modelling Layers

Another objective we want to tackle is to support users in separating the modelling of application-level components from the one of their execution environments (e.g., containers, VMs, etc.). The rationale for this choice is that different users, with different skills and roles, could be focusing on these two aspects. Typically, the application designer will focus on the application structure definition in terms of components and their connections (cf. Figure 2), while an Ops expert will oversee the allocation of components within proper computational elements. The allocation will have to allow the fulfilment of the specified non-functional requirements.

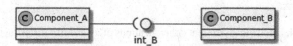

Fig. 2. Modelling the application structure.

Furthermore, given the availability of multiple providers/technologies offering IaaS (Infrastructure-as-a-Service) and, in some cases, compatible PaaS (Platform-as-a-Service) solutions, we want to offer the possibility to provide an abstract definition of the infrastructure (cf. Figure 3) to be used for an application and, then, to define different concretizations of this same infrastructure, so to support deployment and execution of applications into multiple contexts (see the left- and right-hand side of Fig. 4).

For instance, the same components could be made available in two different deployments: an in-house containerized installation to be used for pre-release testing, and a cloud-based non-containerized installation to be used as the main operational environment, resulting into multiple possible mappings of the same abstract computing node.

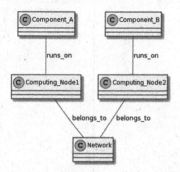

Fig. 3. Modelling an abstract infrastructure and the mapping with components.

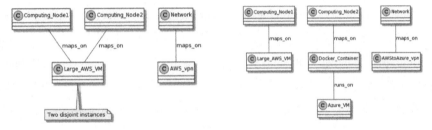

Fig. 4. Modelling different concretizations of an abstract infrastructure.

4   An Example of a DOML Model

Figure 5 shows the skeleton of a simple example of a DOML model, in which a *nginx* web server runs on a VM provisioned by the OpenStack provider. For space constraints, we do not report the whole code. The model is organized in layers. The *application layer* defines the nginx server instance as a software component. The *infrastructure layer* defines a VM connected to a network. The *deployment configuration* states that the nginx instance runs on the VM. Finally, the *concretization layer* defines how components from other layers are mapped to services offered by a specific cloud service provider, in this case OpenStack.

```
doml nginx_openstack

application app {
    software_component nginx {
        properties {...}
    }
}

infrastructure infra {
    vm_image v_img {
        generates vm1
    }
    vm vm1 {
        iface i1 {
            address "16.0.0.1"
            belongs_to net1
        }
    }
    net net1 {
        address "16.0.0.0/24"
        protocol "tcp/ip"
    }
}
```

```
deployment config {
    nginx -> vm1
}

concretizations {
    concrete_infrastructure con {
        provider openstack {
            vm concrete_vm {
                properties {...}
                maps vm1
            }
            vm_image con_vm_image {
                properties {...}
                maps v_img
            }
            net concrete_net {
                properties {...}
                maps net1
            }
        }
    }
    active con
}
```

Fig. 5. Example DOML model of a cloud application running a nginx instance.

5   Discussion

The development of the DOML is an ongoing effort. The first version has been released together with the IaC code generation tool that is able to create Terraform and Ansible scripts. Currently, we are experimenting with the approach through our case studies.

References

1. Morris, K.: Infrastructure as Code: Managing Servers in the Cloud. O'Reilly, Sebastopol (2016)
2. PIACERE. https://www.piacere-project.eu/. Accessed 02 March 2022
3. Terraform. https://www.terraform.io/. Accessed 02 March 2022
4. TOSCA, OASIS Topology and Orchestration Specification for Cloud Applications (TOSCA) TC. OASIS OPEN, OASIS. Accessed 02 March 2022
5. Ansible. https://www.ansible.com/. Accessed 02 March 2022
6. Chef. https://www.chef.io/. Accessed 02 March 2022
7. Puppet. https://puppet.com/. Accessed 02 March 2022
8. Dockerfile. https://docs.docker.com/engine/reference/builder/. Accessed 02 March 2022
9. Kubernetes. https://kubernetes.io/. Accessed 02 March 2022
10. Di Nitto, E.: D3.1 - PIACERE Abstractions, DOML and DOML-E, v1. https://www.piacere-project.eu/public-deliverables. Accessed 02 March 2022

Urban Heat Island Detection Utilizing Citizen Science

Philipp Kisters[(✉)], Vinh Ngu, and Janick Edinger

Universität Hamburg, Mittelweg 177, 20148 Hamburg, Germany
{philipp.kisters,janick.edinger}@uni-hamburg.de,
vinh.ngu@studium.uni-hamburg.de
https://www.inf.uni-hamburg.de/inst/ab/dos.html

Abstract. With rising temperatures and increasing densification in modern cities the risk for so called urban heat islands increases. Urban heat islands pose health risks for elderly people, children, and persons with existing health conditions. Currently, cities rely on satellite images to detect areas of risk since existing sensor networks are not dense enough. However, these measures have either a low spatial or temporal resolution and are not suitable to continuously collect fine-granular data samples. We propose an alternative approach based on a distributed citizen-owned sensor network consisting of existing Smart Home and Internet of Things devices owned by citizens. We further deploy mobile sensors that can be attached to publicly available infrastructure such as buses, rental bikes, or e-scooters. These mobile measurement help to gain temporary insights into areas which have previously not been covered. However, the collected measurements in these areas remains sparse. Therefore, we continuously interpolate the current temperature by utilizing machine learning algorithms. With the existing measurements from mobile sensor stations we train a regression model to learn their dependencies with neighboring stationary weather stations. The predicted weather conditions of unmonitored results in a fine-granular heatmap that allows for an accurate localization of urban heat islands.

Keywords: Citizen science · Smart cities · Distributed services

1 Introduction

Due to the ever-increasing population growth in cities in recent decades, many cities are focusing on the densification of existing residential areas. This often involves building over green areas and thus closing gaps between existing residential buildings [2]. This has negative effects on the residents themselves. First, due to the decreasing number of green spaces, the remaining ones are often perceived as overcrowded and thus reduce the recovering factor [4,6]. Second, decreasing green spaces in favour of asphalt, brick, and concrete increases the absorption of the sun's heat and causes the surface temperature to rise. This leads to an

C. Zirpins et al. (Eds.): ESOCC 2022 Workshops, CCIS 1617, pp. 94–98, 2022.
https://doi.org/10.1007/978-3-031-23298-5_9

elevated risk of areas with significantly higher temperatures than their surroundings [5]. These areas, called urban heat islands (UHI), are an increasing problem in many densely built-up cities and come along with multiple negative effects, including health risks for elderly citizens, children as well as persons with existing health conditions [4,7]. Further, UHIs lead to more energy consumption due to a higher demand for cooling and a decline of water quality in urban areas. This problem is further exacerbated by climate change and the resulting rise in temperatures [4]. In newly build areas, UHIs are considered from the start and taken into account in urban planning. Common countermeasures include the greening of roofs and surfaces as well as the use of water features. Similarly, there are startups[1] emerging which develop products that can be actively used to combat UHIs in existing and upcoming neighborhoods.

However, in order to know where to combat UHIs, areas of risk must first be identified. For this purpose, *Land Surface Temperature* (LST) data is currently used. This data is collected by satellites over entire areas at once. Based on this data, surface temperatures are compared with the surrounding areas, and with repeated data collection, areas of high risks for UHIs can be identified [5]. However, due to their low spatial or temporal resolution, satellites fail to provide continuous, fine-granular data streams.

In this paper, we present an alternative approach to collect temperature data that can be used to detect UHIs. For this purpose, existing citizen-owned sensors from the Smart Home and Internet of Things domain are used and interconnected to create a crowd sensing network. However, these sensors alone would hardly be sufficient to detect local UHIs, as they are sparsely distributed throughout the city. To further increase the coverage of measurement locations we utilize moving sensors which might be attached to public transport or vehicle sharing infrastructure. Measurements taken by these sensors can be used to train a machine learning model that allows to interpolate between stationary sensors and therefore generate a more fine-granular temperature map to detect UHIs. Stationary data can be collected continuously and can be complemented with data from moving sensors to study the development and behavior of UHIs. Likewise, residents can be warned in case of acute high temperatures and short-term countermeasures can be taken.

The remainder of this paper is structured as follows. In Sect. 2 we describe the architecture of the underlying distributed sensor network. In Sect. 3 we present our approach to detect UHIs. We discuss how we interpolate missing sensor data by means of applying moving sensors and detect local UHIs. Finally, we discuss our approach and give a short overview about future steps.

2   System Architecture

Our UHI detection is based on a distributed citizen-managed sensor network that is implemented as a publish subscribe architecture [1]. Citizens who own and operate sensors to collect weather data can provide access to these measurements

---

[1] https://greencitysolutions.de.

in form of continuous data streams. Services, such as the UHI detection, can subscribe to these data streams. This results in a layered architecture as shown in Fig. 1.

The *data layer* consists of the hardware and software to collect, preprocess, store, and provide access to the data. Digital weather stations act as sensors and collect information about atmospheric conditions such as temperature, atmospheric pressure, humidity, wind speed, and solar radiation. Collected data is stored in so-called base stations, which can either be dedicated hardware (e.g., micro computer such as a Raspberry Pi) or a part of an existing computational infrastructure. Base stations run a software that allows individuals to configure not only the data collection but also preprocessing, storage, and sharing options. With this design, all control of the data remains with the citizens who should be able to grant and revoke access rights to their own data streams at any time.

Applications which make use of these data streams and provide valuable services on top of the collected weather data constitute the *service layer*. Services make use of one or several types of weather data in order to perform visualization, aggregation, or forecasting based on this data. As the services might partially or fully depend on data collected by citizens, they need to request access to these data streams. They might also integrate publicly available data sources. As a result of this design, the system consists of n data providers (citizens) and m services with the possibility for each data provider to decide whether an individual service should be able to access its data.

The *network layer* connects data and service layers. It is implemented as a peer-to-peer (P2P) network based on the SkipNet approach [3]. A SkipNet utilizes the lookup efficiency of distributed hash tables and additionally introduces self-selected content IDs that allow for prefix based range queries. We enhanced the content IDs by using an attribute value based naming scheme, that allows not only prefix base range queries but range and selection queries for each attribute value pair. Further, we allow to search for groups of peers by minimizing required search messages.

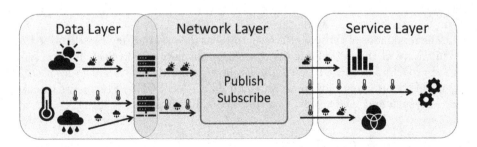

Fig. 1. In the data layer (left), a wide variety of environmental data is collected with the help of multiple sensors. These are connected to their citizen-owned local base stations, which manage access rights and forward collected data to subscribed services (right) via the decentralized publish-subscribe in the network layer (center).

3   UHI Detection

In this paper, we discuss a service that discovers UHIs based on crowdsensed weather data. UHIs can occur very locally due to dense building situations and weather factors such as solar radiation. Although many measuring stations are already operated in current cities, these are not deployed fine-meshed enough to reliably detect UHIs and define their extent. Therefore, it is necessary to obtain additional data from locations that are not covered by stationary measurement stations. Our approach utilizes mobile sensors that can be attached to publicly available infrastructure such as buses, rental curbs, or e-scooters. These mobile data sources cannot provide permanent stationary measurements, but provide snapshots for a particular location at a certain point in time. This spatiotemporal data can enrich data streams from stationary sensors by measurements from areas that previously have not been covered. As these areas get monitored from time to time, each measurement helps to gain a better understanding on local weather dynamics. Figure 2 shows an area that is not covered by stationary sensors (left). Every time a mobile sensor collects data in this area (middle), we gain knowledge which we use to feed our regression model to predict weather conditions at a later point in time when no current measures from this area is available (right).

For our approach it is necessary to identify which features lead to the most accurate predictions with temperature of sensors in close proximity being among the most likely candidates. Other features such as wind speeds, air pressure, and solar radiation of surrounding sensors might be relevant predictors as well. Further, even information unrelated to weather conditions such as time of day and date might be of interest. An area which is exposed to extreme solar radiation at a sunny afternoon in June might have a lower risk of becoming a UHI in August when the afternoon sun is blocked by a building. In experiments, we also need to identify how the number and the density of surrounding sensors affects the accuracy when predicting the temperature and further weather conditions of unmonitored areas.

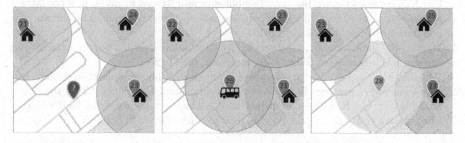

Fig. 2. Some areas are not covered by stationary sensors (left). Whenever mobile sensors collect data in these areas (middle) this knowledge can be used to train a regression model which predicts weather conditions for these unmonitored areas (right).

4 Discussion

Until now, UHIs were detected by repeatedly collecting LST data using satellites which suffer from low temporal or spatial resolution. Our approach provides an alternative that uses a distributed citizen-operated sensor network to detect and locate UHIs in real time. To further increase the resolution of the existing sensor network, mobile sensors are used. Although these measurements do not take place permanently at one location, the occasional measurements at a location can be used to train a machine learning model to continuously predict weather conditions which then allows to predict weather conditions even if no current measurement is available.

In this project, we evaluate to what extent the interpolation between stationary data can be improved with the help of moving sensors and which features need to be chosen to generate the most accurate predictions. Furthermore, we want to automize the detection of UHIs in real time. Therefore, we need to identify expressive characteristics defining an UHI. This might include the *number of sensors* measuring an elevated temperature to avoid outliers and false positives, the absolute *temperature difference* to its surroundings to find areas of risk, and the *time period* over which elevated temperatures need to occur. Additionally, using the fine granular resolution of the collected data, we can better understand the formation and evolution of UHIs and already identify signs of emerging UHIs in order to take countermeasures proactively.

References

1. Bornholdt, H., et al.: SANE: smart networks for urban citizen participation. In: 2019 26th International Conference on Telecommunications (ICT). IEEE (2019)
2. Grêt-Regamey, A., Galleguillos-Torres, M., Dissegna, A., Weibel, B.: How urban densification influences ecosystem services-a comparison between a temperate and a tropical city. Environ. Res. Lett. **15**(7) (2020)
3. Harvey, N.J., Jones, M.B., Saroiu, S., Theimer, M., Wolman, A.: SkipNet: a scalable overlay network with practical locality properties. In: Proceedings of the Fourth USENIX Symposium on Internet Technologies and Systems, vol. 5, p. 9 (2003)
4. Manoli, G., et al.: Magnitude of urban heat islands largely explained by climate and population. Nature **573**(7772) (2019)
5. Martin, P., Baudouin, Y., Gachon, P.: An alternative method to characterize the surface urban heat island. Int. J. Biometeorol. **59**(7) (2015)
6. Wolsink, M.: 'Sustainable city' requires 'recognition'-the example of environmental education under pressure from the compact city. Land Use Policy **52** (2016)
7. Xiao, H., et al.: Responses of urban land surface temperature on land cover: a comparative study of Vienna and Madrid. Sustainability **10**(2) (2018)

Using a Multi-sourced Methodology to Identify Challenges in Software Technologies Research

Juncal Alonso[1]([⊠]) [iD], Leire Orue-Echevarria[1] [iD], Galia Nedeltcheva[2], and Elisabetta Di Nitto[2]

[1] TECNALIA-BRTA, Astondo Bidea 700, 48160 Derio (Bizkaia), Edificio, Spain
juncal.alonso@tecnalia.com
[2] Politecnico di Milano, Piazza Leonardo da Vinci, 32, 20133 Milano, Italy

Abstract. The software industry has a great impact in the European Union's economy as reported in a study by the European Commission [1]. However, in spite of the importance that software has in Europe, there exist several barriers that could hamper its growth. An important one is related to research and development of software technologies, and more specifically the topics that should be funded by the public programmes and policies. The current paper presents a methodology designed with the aim of providing policy-makers with recommendations on the research challenges that should be prioritized. It is a three step methodology, out of which the first one is currently implemented, namely the identification of research topics, taking as input information coming from various sources such as landscape reports, analysis of academic venues, workshops and existing funded-projects. The paper briefly details the main six challenges currently identified in the field of Software Technologies.

Keywords: Research roadmap · Software technologies · Research challenges

1 Introduction

The study "The Economic and Social Impact of Software & Services on Competitiveness and Innovation" by the European Commission reveals that [1]: *"The software industry has a strong economic and social impact throughout the European Union. There is the direct economic contribution from this dynamic industry, its contribution to the wider economy through knowledge spillover and the provision of new technological possibilities, as well as its tremendous effects on society in general."*

The contribution of software and the software-based services (SSBS) industry to the EU economy has been increasing in recent years in every dimension (employment, value added, and productivity) and even though this provides an optimistic landscape, the same study identifies a set of ten barriers in the context of Software Industry that could decrease the growth for the upcoming years, which are: lack of skills, lack of specialized IT and Internet experts, lack of entrepreneurial spirit, missing supporting services, market fragmentation, status-quo orientation of companies, including existing rules and governance structures in IT-using sectors, trust, privacy, security, policy strategies not

© The Author(s), under exclusive license to Springer Nature Switzerland AG 2022
C. Zirpins et al. (Eds.): ESOCC 2022 Workshops, CCIS 1617, pp. 99–103, 2022.
https://doi.org/10.1007/978-3-031-23298-5_10

suited to support ICT innovations, not enough R&D, not enough broadband access, and not enough support for open source software.

To overcome these shortcomings the European Commission presents in the same study, a set of policy initiatives grouped in three categories, deriving in groups of policy related initiatives 1) for a more dynamic user landscape; 2) for better framework conditions; 3) focus on enabling factors. The top 5 policy recommendations are to: enhance e-skills in Europe, support the adoption of ICT in the industry and service sectors, support open source software, increase trust in cloud computing and IT infrastructures, increase public R&D spending in the ICT area.

SWForum.eu [2] intends to support the Commission in their initiatives to resolve these impediments through a strong set of complementary measures that directly and indirectly impact these policy recommendations by: 1) increasing the chances to enhance high level e-skills, bridging the gap between research and industry and contributing to the spread of niche knowledge (cybersecurity, infrastructure, artificial intelligence) between distinct experts promoting cross-fertilization between the areas of software, digital infrastructures, cybersecurity and Artificial Intelligence, 2) creating a self-sustainable forum of researchers and practitioners in the software area, 3) providing guidance to the European Initiatives to improve the Technologies and readiness levels, 4) enhancing the visibility of European based software technology projects, and 5) supporting the Commission policy officers and stakeholders through the creation of the Innovation and research public roadmaps.

The current paper focuses on the activities carried out for the creation of the innovation and research roadmaps in the context of SWForum. It is structured as follows: Sect. 2 describes the roadmapping approach and methodology, while Sect. 3 describes the initial findings, that is, the research challenges identified.

2 Approach and Methodology to Determine the Research Challenges and Recommendations

The methodology followed in SWForum [6] for the roadmap has been organized in three steps, as seen in Fig. 1 and described below. This methodology has already been used in other actions such as HUB4CLOUD [3], which demonstrates the repeatability and the scientific soundness of the approach.

Next, a brief description of the followed methodology is presented:

1. Identification of research challenges from various sources, with a clear definition of the research questions under evaluation in order to limit the scope:

   a. Analysis of publications from the most relevant academic venues (journals and conferences). The search was carried out between June–September 2021. The Top 20 venues with the highest h-index from the Software systems domain. Due to the limited resources of the project only the top 5 publications with the highest number of citations in the timeframe 2016–2021 have been considered. Overall, 100 publications were read initially and 84 further analysed. The publications discarded were so because 1) they were found irrelevant for the chosen topics; 2) the publications were retracted; 3) the search ended in a book chapter.

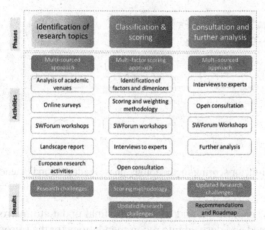

Fig. 1. Methodology followed in SWForum for the roadmapping (adapted and extended from [3]). The current paper focuses on the phase "Identification of research topics".

b. Identification of current and past European Research activities, mainly H2020, in the field of software technologies, digital infrastructures and cybersecurity in the Horizon 2020 topics: ICT-16–2018, ICT-11–2018-2019, ICT-01–2019, ICT-15–2019-2020, ICT-50–2020, ICT-56–2020 and ICT-40–2020.

c. Analysis of the landscape report [4], which included surveys as well as an analysis of existing initiatives such as associations, research roadmaps from other geographical areas, and standards.

d. Analysis of the results of the SWForum workshops [5], especially the second one, devoted to research challenges.

The outcome of this phase is this paper, the first version of the research challenges.

2. Classification and scoring: The classification and scoring methodology (see Fig. 2) aims at providing a first prioritization of the research challenges identified in the previous step. This prioritization will be initially based on a scoring methodology that will be developed taking into consideration several factors such as the timeframe, the impact, the added value for Europe, and more. These factors will be also given a weight taking as input the opinion of subject matter experts. The third step is the scoring, where also input coming from various stakeholders will be included, apart from the initial prioritization based on the scoring methodology. The results will be represented in a graphical manner so that they can be seen easily at a glance. It is important to note that thanks to this methodology it can happen that the software challenges identified in the previous step need to be updated. The outcome of this phase will be a scoring and classification methodology as well as a more detailed set of research challenges. This phase is currently undergoing.

3. Consultation and further and analysis: The initial classification performed will be shared with the constituency through various means such as SWForum workshops,

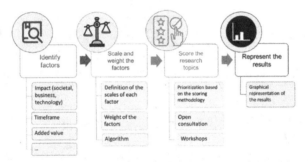

Fig. 2. Multi-factor scoring methodology phases (adapted and extended from [3])

online surveys, interviews, and as such, the final update to the research challenges will be performed and derived into recommendations for the European Commission. The outcome of this phase will be a set of detailed research challenges, discussed with stakeholders as well as a set of recommendations for the European Commission to include as research topics in the upcoming workprogrammes. This phase has not yet started.

3 Identified Research Challenges

The challenges identified following the step 1 are briefly detailed next [6]:

1. Challenge 1: Open Source: popular Open-source software (OSS) software tools are intensively used in both academia and industry for the formal verification of large-scale distributed software and hardware systems. The main challenge relies on investigating the applicability and expressiveness of compliance patterns that need to be introduced in companies' processes as an integral part of the companies' compliance management approach.
2. Challenge 2: Self-repairing and self-healing: Defect prediction and fault localization using artificial intelligence: Bugs are prevalent in software. Many of these defects, including security-related ones, remain unresolved for long periods of time. In order to prevent these defects, there is the need to develop tools, methods and algorithms that would allow an automatic program repair (self-repairing), that is, a software able to translate a specification into a machine-executable activity that would automatically generate a fix for that fault (self-healing). This could be achieved by the development of means for obtaining a semantic representation of programs automatically from the source code, where deep learning algorithms could be later applied.
3. Challenge 3: Continuous software engineering: Delivering the Continuous agenda inspires a number of significant challenges which need to be addressed. Continuous concept has to be perceived when one considers approaches as Enterprise Agile, DevOps, Leann, Beyond Budgeting, and other similar concepts in Lean Thinking. Those philosophies require a holistic and integrated approach across all the activities in the software development lifecycle. As well, it is necessary to be highlighted

the need for tighter connection between the various phases of business strategy, development and execution.

4. Challenge 4: Requirements, Architecture and development: Requirements engineering is a cornerstone of the software development lifecycle. Requirements are expressed in natural language, which often leads to misconceptions, especially when trying to create the conceptual and architectural models of said requirements. NLP is useful here. Deep learning in programming languages, abstractions, semantic representations of syntax of programming languages and (supervised) machine learning algorithms could benefit the quality of the code finally delivered, as code smells and faults can be easier localized and resolved. Finally, new paradigms such as quantum computing will affect the way in which software is developed, where abstractions for modelling, designing and building quantum applications will play a prominent role.

5. Challenge 5: Cybersecurity and privacy: Security is a responsibility of all, not only technical but also organisational. This problem is increasing as the Edge is becoming more popular as edge devices are more prone to be attacked. This challenge includes, among other, issues such as risk assessment in software and network design, use of machine learning for malware detections in libraries and applications of large and complex systems, and data transparency and sharing.

6. Challenge 6: Specific technology domains: The embedded systems and Internet of Things subsector exhibits a massive impact in the ICT sector as an enabling technology for a variety of applications. It creates the possibility to cover basic hardware and software functionality using Open Source Software and Hardware (OSSH) and immediately start at the point of innovation. Other technology domains such as quantum computing will have an impact as already expressed in challenge 4.

References

1. Beckert, B., et al.: European Commission: Directorate-General for Communications Networks, Content and Technology, The economic and social impact of software & services on competitiveness and innovation: final report. Publications Office (2017). https://doi.org/10.2759/949874
2. SwForum Homepage https://www.swforum.eu/. Last accessed 30 March 2022
3. HUB4Cloud consortium. D1.4 Contributing to the European Cloud Computing Strategic Research and Innovation Agenda Q3–2021 (2021)
4. SWForum consortium. D3.1 Landscape report - v1 (2021)
5. SWForum consortium. D2.1 Cross-fertilization workshop report - v1. (2021)
6. SWForum consortium. D3.3 SWForum Research Roadmap – v1 (2021)

ESOCC 2022 Industrial Track

Preface to the ESOCC 2022 Industrial Track

The European Conference on Service-Oriented and Cloud Computing (ESOCC) is among the leading events on advancing the state-of-the-art in services and cloud technologies. It serves as an important venue for scientists as well as practitioners from academia and industry. The main òbjective of the event is to provide a broad forum for the exchange of ideas. To this end, the ESOCC Industrial Track is a forum for the latest achievements of industrial research and development.

For the ESOCC 2022 Industrial Track, invited experts have carefully selected the contributions based on at least 2 single-blind reviews. In the end, the track included one high quality paper focussing on "Monitoring for Cloud Environments".

November 2022   ESOCC Co-Chairs

Organization

ESOCC 2022 Industrial Track Chair

Andreas Both   Anhalt University of Applied Sciences, Germany

Rethinking Monitoring for Cloud Environments: BMC Software AIOps Case Study

Sai Eswar Garapati[1,2], Erhan Giral[1,2], and Smiljana Antonijević[1,2](✉) 🆔

[1] BMC Software, Santa Clara, USA
smiljana_antonijevic@bmc.com
[2] BMC Software, 2103 CityWest Boulevard, Houston, TX 77042, USA

Abstract. This paper presents the experiences, insights, and solutions resulting from the development of BMC AIOps, a SaaS solution from BMC Software, Inc. (BMC) that applies machine learning and predictive capabilities across IT operations and DevOps environments for real-time, enterprise-wide observability, insights, and automated remediation. We first briefly chronicle the evolution of this product, and then focus on our service-centric perspective on noise reduction and root cause analysis based on incremental differential clustering for causality, and a novel clustering algorithm that BMC built to tackle service models that have thousands of services and millions of devices, and where root cause analysis needs to be performed in near real time.

Keywords: AIOPs · Enterprise-wide observability · Service-centric noise reduction · Incremental differential clustering for causality · Root cause analysis

1 Introduction

The complex and dynamic nature of today's cloud-based distributed applications have overwhelmed traditional, siloed monitoring approaches. To address this gap, DevOps practitioners and Site Reliability Engineering (SRE) teams are increasingly exploring artificial intelligence (AI) and machine learning (ML) as means to detect and predict problems faster, while recommending automated recovery and remediation steps. Cloud application development and deployment has been simplified, while cloud-based distributed application monitoring and operations are still complex.

In addressing these challenges, BMC Software, Inc. (BMC) is developing a modern SaaS solution that applies machine learning and predictive capabilities across IT operations and DevOps environments for real-time, enterprise-wide observability, insights, and automated remediation. Now in its second year of development, BMC AIOps is an award-winning solution,[1] which has started where good product development should always start—with users and their needs—and it has continued to grow, change, and adapt through a constant dialog between BMC's interdisciplinary product team and its users.

---

[1] BMC AIOps was awarded "Best Overall AI Solution" in the annual AI Breakthrough Awards program for 2021 (see: https://aibreakthroughawards.com/2021-winners/).

© The Author(s), under exclusive license to Springer Nature Switzerland AG 2022
C. Zirpins et al. (Eds.): ESOCC 2022 Workshops, CCIS 1617, pp. 109–115, 2022.
https://doi.org/10.1007/978-3-031-23298-5_11

In this paper, we share our experiences, insights, and solutions resulting from the development of BMC's AIOps. We first briefly chronicle the evolution of the product, and then focus on one of its key elements – automated root cause analysis (RCA).

1.1 BMC AIOps – Background

Our AIOps solution is built on BMC's Autonomous Digital Enterprise platform, which was launched in 2019. In early 2020, BMC' engineers, data scientists, and product managers began charting the AIOps technical and business contours. Soon after, UX designers picked it up, visualizing those initial contours in the prototypes our researchers presented to BMC software users.

AIOps user research began in September of 2020, and it included several iterative phases. The study comprised of seventy-six users from thirty-six strategic customers representing several major industry groups that provide cloud or IT products and/or services. The participants included executives, system admins, service portfolio leads, VPs of cloud products, IT technical directors, principal technical architects, software developers, process advisers, DevOps team members, as well as SREs and performance engineers. In the first set of user research sessions, we sought to understand users' current practices, challenges, and needs related to root cause analysis and event noise reduction. Based on identified user needs, we developed initial solutions for transforming users' predominantly manual practices into modern and efficient AI/ML-based solutions.

These initial solutions were tested with users and iteratively improved based on user feedback. Finally, we continued adding and testing with users further functionalities such as online collaborative features, automated remediation, and so on. The study yielded more than a hundred hours of recorded user interviews, providing us with a wealth of valuable and actionable insights.

In terms of root cause analysis, one of our first goals was to learn whether our customers differentiated between root cause and probable cause, and—if so—what was the differentiator. Across customers and user types, the agreement was that probable cause allows users to explore the nature of data giving a probability of what might be the root cause. Pertaining to the visual display of root cause information, users identified service model topology as the most important element of the BMC AIOps solution: "It comes right to the root causes, and it shows the relationship in the impacted path, so this is everything I would have expected to see", one user commented.

Related to event noise reduction, we learned that users employ a set of techniques, from simplistic versions of deduplication and correlation through tacit knowledge to more advanced correlation approaches. Efforts such as clustering events and collating sites to reduce the number of alerts and modify their priority, or filtering out noise through the normalization and enrichment processes, have mostly been done manually, but automation is increasingly desired. Our customers thus enthusiastically embraced the prospect of AI/ML based noise reduction.

Yet uncertainties about the actual results and feasibility lingered, stemming from customers' uneven maturity, the awareness of general AI/ML limitations, as well as from the need to better understand what is considered noise and what would be algorithmically discarded and/or combined to reduce noise. As one user put it: "Noise reduction based on AI is the Holy Grail from a service provider perspective. But how do you do that?".

One of our answers to this question was the service centric perspective on noise reduction, which we detail in the following section.

2   A Service Centric Perspective on Noise Reduction

Not every anomaly, outlier or even failure is necessarily a problem that leads to business interruption. In fact, in a sufficiently complex environment there is always some background event load, almost like the constant, cosmic background noise. Some of these events, however, are leading indicators that turn into problems with real business impact.

In the past, various attempts have been made to reduce the noise operators face by using online or offline event processing algorithms that relied on event similarities to calculate correlations. Such techniques, however, often fall short in noise reduction because correlation does not necessarily mean causation. Also, most proposed techniques involve heavy hyperparameter tuning that simply pushes the model accuracy responsibility to the end users. The traditional way to cluster events is to identify correlation based on text/time and apply partitioning based clustering like K-Means with configured K [1]. There are others in the industry who employed a configuration threshold based on density and spectral clustering using correlations identified from textual and service domains which suffer from manual tuning and lack of causality issues.

But let's first identify what is noise. There are different kinds of noise events:

- Short Term Flapping Events: These are the events that constantly transition between the critical state and the normal state in a short period. These alarms are commonly generated due to disturbances on metrics configured with alarms, primarily when the metrics are operating nearer to their thresholds.
- Long Term Flapping Alarms: Repeating alarms frequently make transitions between critical and non-critical states with more extended periods. These are generated by repeated on-off actions on devices or regular oscillatory disturbances in metrics.
- Standing Alarms: Another set of noise alarms are standing alarms or alarms that remain in an active state for a prolonged duration. The primary reason for these alarms is typically the inefficiencies in operations and maintenance.
- Alarm Storms/Floods: Finally, Alarm Floods occur when an abnormal situation occurs in some environment. The fault may spread to many other places through interconnections between devices and process units. These are the most important groups of alarms that signify any abnormality in the environment and contain the root cause and huge alarms from the affected components.

BMC believes that if we are to reduce the noise maximally, establishing causal relationships between events should be the goal. Such an endeavor would be best informed if the target service is first modelled for its known components (sources of events) and their transactional, as well as resource dependencies.

There are three integrated layers of topology data contained in our AIOps Solution. The topmost layer contains the connections between software components; for example, it captures the calling relationships between front-end servers and back-end servers. The Middle layer contains Infrastructure topology data between different Virtualized and

Physical Infrastructures like relationships between Containers and Virtual Machines. The Third Layer contains the Network infrastructure, including relationships between networking components like switches and routers. All these layers are connected across to give the IT infrastructure a combined topology.

That kind of modelling would have been an uphill battle in the past, as such descriptive models are often brittle. However, today's observability landscape is rich with tools and methodologies that allow us to collect near-real-time topological data from all layers of business services, all the way from end user workflows down to the network and infrastructure topologies that these workflows exercise. The difficult part, though, is to integrate the topologies that have different ontologies into a coherent knowledge graph that can catalog transactional and resource dependencies in an environment such that analysis algorithms can be situationally aware about the sources of these events.

We create a knowledge graph of the IT Infrastructure domain. The knowledge graph contains known relationships across different monitored entities for which metrics and events are collected. The knowledge graph uses a graph-based data model to represent domain knowledge. This framework allows us to capture data from experts manually or through machine learning. The knowledge graph is a directed labelled graph. Nodes and edges have a well-defined meaning. In our data model, a node represents entities, and edges represent relation. Furthermore, BMC's ADE platform features a vendor agnostic, integrative connector framework that allows us to build on rich topological information, no matter what the observability stack is composed of in the environment.

3   Incremental Differential Clustering for Causality

We believe maximal event noise reduction is only possible when events are sorted based on causality; once ordered for causality, it is trivial to separate the root cause events from symptomatic events that have transpired on the same dependency chain after the root cause event. Furthermore, when the causal chains are grouped by the root cause event, seemingly unrelated but causally linked incidents are corelated. Hence, we postulate that identification of the root cause ought to offer the best possible reduction of noise.

For this reason, the BMC team built a novel clustering algorithm that leverages observed topologies to reason about causal distances of event pairs by relying on observed and ontological distances of the sources of these events to cluster causally linked events together. We make no assumption about the size and number of these clusters, but rely on the topology to guide us to autotune our clustering. The resulting algorithm thus requires zero maintenance from the user both in terms of data modelling as well as in terms of hyperparameter tuning or training.

Our clustering relies on a knowledge graph that graphically maintains various domain-specific bits of knowledge, so that we can reason about the encountered events with ontological inference. This allows us to generalize what is known about anomalies in technologies and frameworks into cause-and-effect transmission conduits that point us to the root cause. A situation/cluster comprises events associated with the same or different host that are aggregated based on their occurrence, message, topology, or a combination of these factors. Events are collected from multiple sources across infrastructure, application, and network resources available from various monitoring solution vendors. If we can identify the noise into a group and identify the root cause, we consider it a success, as mentioned earlier.

Pairwise event comparison sounds expensive, and it is. Any naïve approach to pairwise event evaluation will yield quadratic runtime; hence we employ a small world approximation on the service graph while computing the causal distances between event pairs. Since the service models we tackle often have thousands of services and millions of devices, and root cause analysis needs to be performed in near real time, using a small world approximation keeps our comparison space in check (Fig. 1).

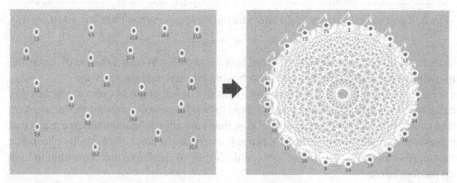

Fig. 1. Events depicted as nodes (left); all possible causal links between these events as K21 (right).

This conversion ensures we scale in logarithmic time complexity, as opposed to the quadratic time complexity of naïve pairwise causal distance evaluation. This technique gives us the ability to incrementally add and delete events in real time. It also acts as a regularizer by subsampling the data in a multi-layered fashion, reducing noise further in the process. We found that this approximation improves our accuracy, and, most likely due to the spatial locality it implies, is not a compromise. The dense graph is transformed into a Delaunay graph retaining long range links along with short range links, and it is further processed to extract the minimum arborescence tree. The arborescence tree is then used to identify the optimum distances where the differential clustering algorithm can recognize all possible graph cuts and identify the natural rate of change for the graph separation. This extracted tree exposes the natural characteristics of the graph and its distances to all nodes in directed paths (Fig. 2).

We track the rate of change on these trees to gauge how active it really is, as an operator would be interested in separating active emerging cases from dormant (perhaps mitigated) cases. We then find the cluster boundaries using causal distances by calculating the rate of change of their causal distances. Those directed clusters that are naturally stable for longer causal distances are retained and otherwise merged into a much more stable directed cluster. Finally, the resulting clusters indicate active situations and all their causally related events ordered by causality.

Note that this approach enables us to handle changes in the distribution and scale of the events without any manual tuning and to adapt in a dynamic fashion. At the same

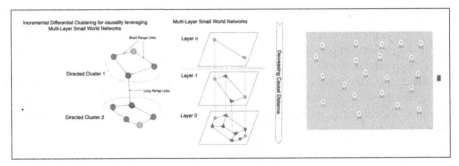

Fig. 2. Event causality search space after small world approximation Delaunay graph (right).

time, we will be able to identify directed clusters at different causal distances according to underlying event distribution in a much more intuitive and natural way.

Each of these clusters now represent a causally linked graph of event signatures. We call these structures Situations and use them to build a narrative around the incident, its root cause, and impact. Since the event signatures are already maintained as a graph that represents causality, finding the root cause is essentially a network centrality check that maximizes causality, and we use a trivial derivative of the PageRank algorithm to look up the root cause.

We invented a directed clustering algorithm to form a directed causal event graph from the causal scores measured from the events and their features. After that, we employed a custom version of Eigenvector centrality measures to achieve Probable RCA scores over the causal event graph. Each cluster can be visually shown as below with edge scores showing causal scores and node scores showing RCA scores (Fig. 3).

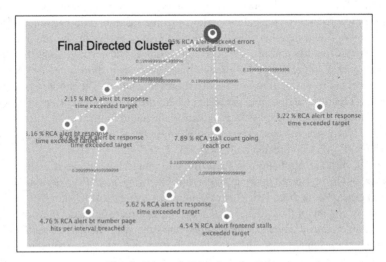

Fig. 3. Directed clustering algorithm.

Each of these Situations is presented in the user interface (UI) as shown below (Fig. 4).

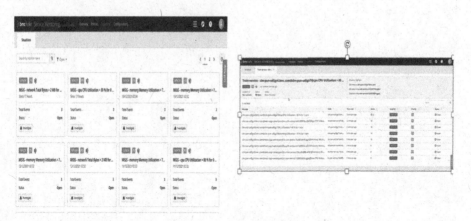

Fig. 4. Situations in the BMC AIOPs UI.

When users investigate each Situation, they see all the symptomatic events and probable root causes grouped together in the sorting order of a RCA score, which signifies the probability of that event being the root cause candidate.

Our solutions for service-centric noise reduction and for incremental differential clustering for causality were presented to users in a series of research studies conducted between March and December 2021. Probable Cause Analysis was very well received and evaluated as a "major saver". While the term "Situations" was not familiar or intuitive to the users, the presented solution for having the BMC AIOps software automatically group and correlate events was assessed as "incredibly helpful" and "a very useful point of view".

Towards the end of 2021, the BMC AIOps solution was initially rolled out to the first set of customers. Our next steps are to test and evaluate BMC AIOps in customers' environments, and to continue developing and perfecting it through continuous user research engagement.

Reference

1. Shi, N., Liu, X., Guan, Y.: An improved k-means clustering algorithm. In: 2010 Third International Symposium on Intelligent Information Technology and Security Informatics. 9th International Proceedings on Proceedings. IEEE, Jian (2010)

Author Index

Printed in the United States
by Baker & Taylor Publisher Services